CON

2 **BOBBLE-LICIOUS PILLOW**

4 **100 MOTIF AFGHAN**

8 **CLUTTER CATCHER BASKETS**

10 **BOLD ANGLES PILLOW**

12 **GEOMETRIC WALL HANGING**

14 **COLORFUL COGS AFGHAN & PILLOW SET**

18 **BOUQUET BASKETS**

20 **BRIGHT SQUARES BLANKET & PILLOW**

23 **COTTON DISHCLOTH**

24 **CITRUS SLICE RUG**

26 **GINGHAM PICNIC BLANKET**

28 **HANDY BASKET**

30 **FULL CIRCLE PILLOW**

32 **FLOWER POWER TABLE RUNNER**

36 **COLOR WHEEL PILLOW**

38 **HOT HIBISCUS TEA COZY**

41 **ZIGZAG BLANKET**

42 **RAINBOW STRIPES TABLET & PHONE CASES**

45 **SPECTRUM AFGHAN**

46 **SPIKE-STITCH PILLOW**

48 **POP ART FLOWERS BLANKET**

51 **FLOWER POT COZY**

52 **STRIPED PLACE SETTING**

54 **LARKSFOOT BLANKET**

56 **CHARTS & DIAGRAMS**

BOBBLE-LICIOUS PILLOW

Easy

MEASUREMENTS
Approx 20"/51cm square

MATERIALS
Yarn (4)

Patons® *Canadiana*™, 3½oz/100g balls, each approx 205yd/187m (acrylic)
- 5 balls in #10628 Tangy or #10413 Raspberry or #10610 Fool's Gold

Hook
- Size H/8 (5mm) crochet hook, *or size needed to obtain gauge*

Notion
- 20"/51cm square pillow form

GAUGE
14 dc and 7 rows = 4"/10cm using size H/8 (5mm) hook.
TAKE TIME TO CHECK GAUGE.

STITCH GLOSSARY
Bobble (Yoh and draw up a loop. Yoh and draw through 2 loops on hook) 5 times in indicated stitch. Yoh and draw through all loops on hook.

FRONT and BACK (Make alike)
Ch 68.

1st row: (WS) 1 dc in 4th ch from hook (counts as 2 dc). 1 dc in each ch to end of chain. Turn. 66 dc.

2nd row: Ch 1. 1 sc in each of first 3 dc. Bobble in next dc. *1 sc in each of next 3 dc. Bobble in next dc. Rep from * to last 2 sts. 1 sc in each of last 2 sts. Turn.

3rd row: Ch 3 (counts as dc). 1 dc in each st to end of row. Turn.

4th row: Ch 1. 1 sc in each of first 5 dc. Bobble in next dc. *1 sc in each of next 3 dc. Bobble in next dc. Rep from * to last 4 sts. 1 sc in each of last 4 sts. Turn.

5th row: Ch 3 (counts as dc). 1 dc in each st to end of row. Turn.

Rep last 4 rows for pat until work from beg measures approx 20"/51cm, ending on a RS row. Fasten off.

Joining Front and Back
1st rnd: With WS facing each other, join yarn with sl st to any corner st of Pillow. Ch 1. *Working through both thicknesses,* work sc evenly around 3 sides of Pillow, having 3 sc in each corner. Insert pillow form. Complete rnd of sc. Join with sl st to first sc.

2nd rnd: Ch 1. *Working from left to right, instead of from right to left as usual,* work 1 reverse sc in each sc around. Join with sl st to first sc. Fasten off.•

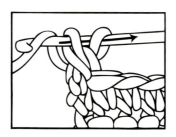 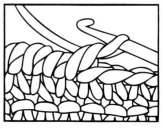

REVERSE SINGLE CROCHET

100 MOTIF AFGHAN

Easy

MEASUREMENTS
Approx 47½"/120.5cm x 62½"/158.5cm

MATERIALS
Yarn (4)

Caron® *Simply Soft*®, 6 oz/170g balls, each approx 315yd/288m (acrylic)
- 1 ball in #9762 Burgundy (A)
- 1 ball in #9763 Harvest Red (B)
- 1 ball in #B9604 Watermelon (C)
- 1 ball in #B9605 Mango (D)
- 1 ball in #9778 Orange (E)
- 1 ball in #9782 Gold (F)
- 1 ball in #9771 Chartreuse (G)
- 1 ball in #9779 Green (H)
- 1 ball in #9770 Cool Green (I)
- 1 ball in #B9608 Blue Mint (J)
- 1 ball in #9784 Cobalt Blue (K)
- 1 ball in #9767 Royal Blue (L)
- 1 ball in #B9609 Berry Blue (M)
- 1 ball in #9781 Purple (N)
- 1 ball in #9764 Fuchsia (O)

Hook
- Size H/8 (5mm) crochet hook, *or size needed to obtain gauge*

GAUGE
13 sc and 14 rows = 4"/10cm using size H/8 (5mm) hook.
Small motif = approx 2½"/6cm square.
Medium motif = approx 5"/12.5cm square.
Large motif = approx 7½"/19cm square.
TAKE TIME TO CHECK GAUGE.

STITCH GLOSSARY
Beg bobble Ch 3. (Yoh and draw up a loop. Yoh and draw through 2 loops on hook) twice in indicated stitch. Yoh and draw through all loops on hook.
Bobble (Yoh and draw up a loop. Yoh and draw through 2 loops on hook) 3 times in indicated stitch. Yoh and draw through all loops on hook.

NOTE
- Ch 3 at beg of rnd counts as dc throughout.

LARGE MOTIF (Make 2 of each color—30 total)
See Diagram 1 on page 7. Ch 4. Join with sl st to first ch to form a ring.

1st rnd: (Beg bobble. Ch 1. Bobble) in ring. (Ch 3. Bobble. Ch 1. Bobble) 3 times in ring. Ch 3. Join with sl st to top of beg bobble.

2nd rnd: Sl st to next ch-1 sp. (Beg bobble. Ch 1. Bobble) in same sp as last sl st. *Ch 3. (1 dc. Ch 3) twice in next ch-3 sp for corner. (Bobble. Ch 1. Bobble) in next ch-1 sp. Rep from * twice more. Ch 3. (1 dc. Ch 3) twice in last ch-3 sp for corner. Join with sl st to top of beg bobble.

3rd rnd: Sl st to next ch-1 sp. (Beg bobble. Ch 1. Bobble) in same sp as last sl st. *Ch 1. 1 dc in next ch-3 sp. Ch 3. (1 dc. Ch 3) twice in next corner ch-3 sp. 1 dc in next ch-3 sp. Ch 1.** (Bobble. Ch 1. Bobble) in next ch-1 sp. Rep from * twice more, then from * to ** once. Join with sl st to top of beg bobble.

4th rnd: Sl st to next ch-1 sp. (Beg bobble. Ch 1. Bobble) in same sp as last sl st. *Ch 3. Skip next ch-1 sp. 1 dc in next ch-3 sp. Ch 3. (1 dc. Ch 3) twice in next corner ch-3 sp. 1 dc in next ch-3 sp. Ch 3. Skip next ch-1 sp.** (Bobble. Ch 1. Bobble) in next ch-1 sp. Rep from * twice more, then from * to ** once. Join with sl st to top of beg bobble.

5th rnd: Sl st to next ch-1 sp. (Beg bobble. Ch 1. Bobble) in same sp as last sl st. *Ch 1. 1 dc in next ch-3 sp. Ch 3. 1 dc in next ch-3 sp. Ch 3. (1 dc. Ch 3) twice in next corner ch-3 sp. Ch 3.

100 MOTIF AFGHAN

1 dc in next ch-3 sp. Ch 1.** (Bobble. Ch 1. Bobble) in next ch-1 sp. Rep from * twice more, then from * to ** once. Join with sl st to top of beg bobble.

6th rnd: Sl st to next ch-1 sp. (Beg bobble. Ch 1. Bobble) in same sp as last sl st. *Ch 3. Skip next ch-1 sp. (1 dc in next ch-3 sp. Ch 3) twice. (1 dc. Ch 3) twice in next corner ch-3 sp. (1 dc in next ch-3 sp. Ch 3) twice. Skip next ch-1 sp.** (Bobble. Ch 1. Bobble) in next ch-1 sp. Rep from * twice more, then from * to ** once. Join with sl st to top of beg bobble. 7th rnd: Ch 1. 1 sc in same sp as last sl st. 1 sc in next ch-1 sp. 1 sc in next bobble. *(3 sc in next ch-3 sp. Skip next dc) 3 times. (2 sc. Ch 3. 2 sc) in next corner ch-3 sp. (3 sc in next ch-3 sp. Skip next dc) twice. 3 sc in next ch-3 sp.** 1 sc in next bobble. 1 sc in next ch-1 sp. 1 sc in next bobble. Rep from * twice more, then from * to ** once. Join with sl st to first sc. Fasten off.

MEDIUM MOTIF (Make 3 of each color—45 total)

See Diagram 2 on page 7. Ch 4. Join with sl st to first ch to form a ring.

1st rnd: Ch 3. [2 dc. (Ch 3. 3 dc) 3 times] all in ring. Ch 1. Join with hdc to top of ch 3.

2nd rnd: Ch 3. 2 dc around post of hdc. [(3 dc. Ch 3. 3 dc) in next ch-3 sp] 3 times. 3 dc in same sp as first 3 dc. Ch 1. Join with hdc to top of ch 3.

3rd rnd: Ch 3. 2 dc around post of hdc. *3 dc between next 2 groups of 3 dc. (3 dc. Ch 3. 3 dc) in next ch-3 sp. Rep from * twice more. 3 dc between next 2 groups of 3 dc. 3 dc in same sp as first 3 dc. Ch 1. Join with hdc to top of ch 3.

4th rnd: Ch 3. 2 dc around post of hdc. *(3 dc between next 2 groups of 3 dc) twice. (3 dc. Ch 3. 3 dc) in next ch-3 sp. Rep from * twice more. (3 dc between next 2 groups of 3 dc) twice. 3 dc in same sp as first 3 dc. Ch 1. Join with hdc to top of ch 3.

5th rnd: Ch 1. 2 sc around post of hdc. (1 sc in each of next 12 dc. 5 sc in next ch-3 sp) 3 times. 1 sc in each of next 12 dc. 3 sc in same sp as first sc. Join with sl st to first sc. Fasten off.

SMALL MOTIF (Make 2 each with A, B, C, D, E, F, H, I, K, M and N. Make 1 with G, J and L—25 total)

See Diagram 3. Ch 4. Join with sl st to first ch to form a ring.

1st rnd: Ch 3. [2 dc. (Ch 3. 3 dc) 3 times] all in ring. Ch 1. Join with hdc to top of ch 3. 2nd rnd: Ch 3. 1 dc around post of hdc. [1 dc in each of next 3 dc. (2 dc. Ch 3. 2 dc) in next ch-3 sp] 3 times. 1 dc in each of next 3 dc. 2 dc in same sp as first sc. Ch 3. Join with sl st to top of ch 3. Fasten off.

FINISHING

Following Assembly Diagram, sew Motifs tog.

Edging

1st rnd: (RS) Join H with sl st to any corner. Ch 2 (does not count as hdc). Work 1 hdc in each st around, having 3 hdc in each corner. Join with sl st to first hdc. Fasten off.

2nd rnd: Join I with sl st to any corner hdc. Ch 1. 1 sc in each hdc around, having 3 sc in each corner hdc. Join with sl st to first sc. Fasten off.

3rd rnd: Join J with sl st to any corner sc. Ch 1. 1 sc in each sc, having 3 sc in each corner sc. Join with sl st to first sc. Fasten off.

4th rnd: With K, as 3rd rnd. Fasten off. •

ASSEMBLY DIAGRAM

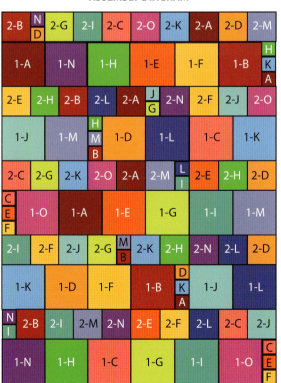

DIAGRAM 1

LARGE MOTIF

DIAGRAM 2

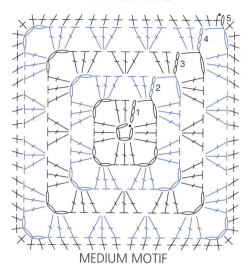

MEDIUM MOTIF

DIAGRAM 3

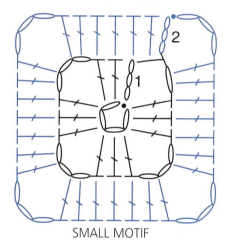

SMALL MOTIF

STITCH KEY

⌒ = chain (ch)

• = slip st (sl st)

+ = single crochet (sc)

T = half double crochet (hdc)

╪ = double crochet (dc)

⧨ = Beg bobble

⧫ = Bobble

7

CLUTTER CATCHER BASKETS

Easy

MEASUREMENTS

Small Basket
Approx 10"/25.5cm in diameter x 6"/15cm tall

Medium Basket
Approx 12"/30.5cm in diameter x 7"/18cm tall

Large Basket
Approx 14"/35.5cm in diameter 8"/20.5cm tall

MATERIALS

Yarn
Bernat® Blanket Brights™, 10½oz/300g balls, each approx 220yd/201m (polyester)

Small Basket
• 2 balls in #12002 Carrot Orange

Medium Basket
• 2 balls in #12008 Pixie Pink

Large Basket
• 3 balls in #12007 Pow Purple

Hook
• Size M/N-13 (9mm) crochet hook, *or size needed to obtain gauge*

Notion
• 1 stitch marker

GAUGE

7 sc and 7 rows = 4"/10cm with 2 strands held together using size M/N-13 (9mm) hook.
TAKE TIME TO CHECK GAUGE.

NOTES

• The instructions are written for smallest size. If changes are necessary for larger size(s) the instructions will be written thus ( ).
• Join all rnds with sl st to first sc.

BASKET

With 2 strands held tog, ch 2.

1st rnd: 8 sc in 2nd ch from hook. Join.
2nd rnd: Ch 1. 3 sc in each sc around. Join. 24 sc.
3rd rnd: Ch 1. *2 sc in next sc. 1 sc in next sc. Rep from * around. Join. 36 sc.
4th rnd: Ch 1. *2 sc in next sc. 1 sc in each of next 2 sc. Rep from * around. Join. 48 sc.
5th rnd: Ch 1. *2 sc in next sc. 1 sc in each of next 3 sc. Rep from * around. Join. 60 sc.

Sizes Medium and Large Only

6th rnd: Ch 1. *2 sc in next sc. 1 sc in each of next 4 sc. Rep from * around. Join. 72 sc.
7th rnd: Ch 1. *2 sc in next sc. 1 sc in each of next 5 sc. Rep from * around. Join. 84 sc.

Size Large Only

8th rnd: Ch 1. *2 sc in next sc. 1 sc in each of next 6 sc. Rep from * around. Join. 96 sc.
9th rnd: Ch 1. *2 sc in next sc. 1 sc in each of next 7 sc. Rep from * around. Join. 108 sc.

All Sizes

Next rnd: Ch 1. Working into back loops only, 1 sc in each sc around. Join. Place marker at end of rnd.
Next rnd: Ch 1. Working into both loops, 1 sc in each sc around. Join. Rep last rnd until work from marked rnd measures 5 (6–8)"/12.5 (15–20.5)cm. Do not fasten off.
Next rnd (Handle openings): Ch 1. 1 sc in each of next 12 (17–22) sc. Ch 1. Skip next sc. 1 sc in each of next 4 (6–8) sc. Ch 1. Skip next sc. 1 sc in each of next 24 (34–44) sc. Ch 1. Skip next sc. 1 sc in each of next 4 (6–8) sc. Ch 1. Skip next sc. 1 sc in each sc to end of rnd. Join.
Next rnd: Ch 1. 1 sc in each sc and ch-1 sp around. Join.
Next rnd: Ch 1. 1 sc in each sc around. Join. Fasten off.

Handles

With 2 strands tog, ch 18 (22–26). Thread chain in through 1st ch-1 sp of Handle opening rnd and back out through 2nd ch-1 sp of same rnd. Join with sl st to first ch to form ring, being careful not to twist.

1st rnd: Ch 1. 1 sc in each ch around, rotating chain through Handle opening for ease of working. Join. Fasten off. Rep for second Handle.•

BOLD ANGLES PILLOW

Intermediate

MEASUREMENTS
Approx 18"/45.5cm square

MATERIALS
Yarn
Bernat® Super Value™, 7oz/197g balls, each approx 426yd/389m (acrylic)
- 1 ball in #00616 Peacock (A)
- 1 ball in #53223 Grass (B)
- 1 ball in #00607 Berry (C)
- 1 ball in #07711 Navy (D)

Hook
- Size H/8 (5mm) crochet hook, *or size needed to obtain gauge*

Notion
- Pillow form, 18"/46cm square

GAUGE
13 sc and 14 rows = 4"/10cm using size H/8 (5mm) crochet hook.
TAKE TIME TO CHECK GAUGE.

NOTE
- Use separate balls of yarn for each area of color in the design. When joining colors, work to last 2 loops on hook of first color. Draw new color through last 2 loops and proceed.

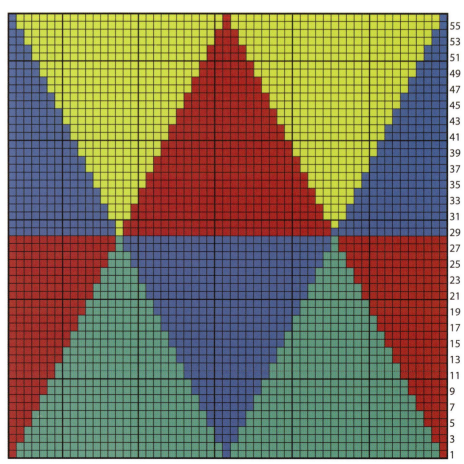

Start here

PILLOW FRONT

With B, ch 58.

1st row: (RS) 1 sc in 2nd ch from hook. 1 sc in each ch to end of chain. Turn. 57 sc.

2nd row: Ch 1. 1 sc in each sc to end of row. Turn. Work Chart in sc until 56th row of Chart is complete, reading RS rows from right to left and WS rows from left to right and joining A at end of last row.

Next 2 rows: With A, ch 1. 1 sc in each sc to end of row. Turn.

Fasten off at end of last row.

PILLOW BACK

With D, ch 58.

1st row: (RS) 1 sc in 2nd ch from hook. 1 sc in each ch to end of chain. Turn. 57 sc.

2nd row: Ch 1. 1 sc in each sc to end of row. Turn. Rep last row until Back measures same as Front. Fasten off.

FINISHING

Holding WS of Front and Back tog and working through both thicknesses, join D with sl st in corner. Ch 1. Work sc evenly around, having 3 sc in each corner and inserting pillow form before joining 4th side. Join with sl st to first sc. Fasten off.•

GEOMETRIC WALL HANGING

Easy

MEASUREMENTS
Approx 24"/61cm x 36"/91.5cm, excluding fringe

MATERIALS
Yarn (4)

Lily® *Sugar'n Cream*®, 2½oz/71g balls, each approx 120yd/109m (cotton)
- 3 balls in #01215 Robins Egg (A)
- 2 balls in #00004 Ecru (B)
- 2 balls in #00073 Sunshine (C)
- 5 balls in #00095 Red (D)
- 3 balls in #00002 Black (E)

Hook
- Size F/5 (3.75mm) crochet hook, *or size needed to obtain gauge*

Notion
- Dowel or branch for hanging

GAUGES
15 sc and 16 rows = 4"/10cm using size F/5 (3.75mm) hook.
Square Motif = approx 6"/15cm square.
TAKE TIME TO CHECK GAUGE.

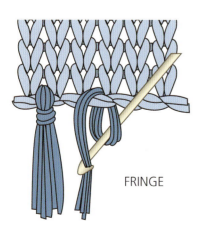
FRINGE

WALL HANGING
Square Motif

Make 3 with D as Color 1 and C as Color 2.
Make 3 with A as Color 1 and C as Color 2.
Make 3 with E as Color 1 and A as Color 2.
Make 1 with D as Color 1 and C as Color 2.
Make 1 with B as Color 1 and D as Color 2.
Make 4 with E as Color 1 and B as Color 2.
Make 3 with A as Color 1 and B as Color 2.
With Color 1, ch 2.

**1st row: (RS) 3 sc in 2nd ch from hook. Turn.
2nd to 5th rows: Ch 1. 2 sc in first sc. 1 sc in each sc to last sc. sc. 2 sc in last sc. Turn. 11 sc at end of 5th row.
6th row: Ch 1. 1 sc in each sc to end of row. Turn.
7th to 11th rows: Ch 1. 2 sc in first sc. 1 sc in each sc to last sc. 2 sc in last sc. Turn. 21 sc at end of 11th row.
12th row: As 6th row.
13th to 17th rows: Ch 1. 2 sc in first sc. 1 sc in each sc to last sc. 2 sc in last sc. Turn. 31 sc at end of 17th row.
18th row: As 6th row.** Join Color 2. Break Color 1.
19th row: With Color 2, as 6th row.
20th to 24th rows: Ch 1. Sc2tog. 1 sc in each sc to last 2 sc. Sc2tog. Turn. 21 sts at end of 24th row.
25th row: As 6th row.
26th to 30th rows: Ch 1. Sc2tog. 1 sc in each sc to last 2 sc. Sc2tog. Turn. 11 sts at end of 30th row.
31st row: As 6th row.
32nd to 35th rows: Ch 1. Sc2tog. 1 sc in each sc to last 2 sc. Sc2tog. Turn. 3 sts at end of 35th row.
36th row: Ch 1. Sc3tog. Fasten off.

Triangle Motif (make 4)
With D, ch 2. Work from ** to ** as given for Square Motif. Fasten off.

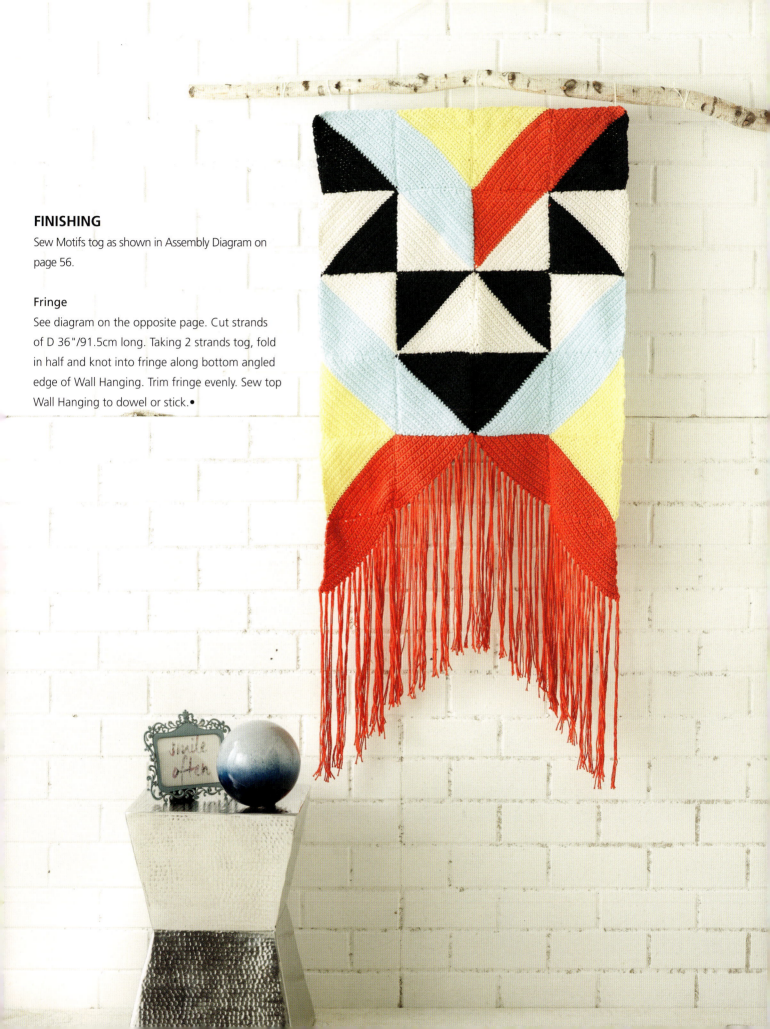

FINISHING
Sew Motifs tog as shown in Assembly Diagram on page 56.

Fringe
See diagram on the opposite page. Cut strands of D 36"/91.5cm long. Taking 2 strands tog, fold in half and knot into fringe along bottom angled edge of Wall Hanging. Trim fringe evenly. Sew top Wall Hanging to dowel or stick.•

COLORFUL COGS AFGHAN & PILLOW SET

Intermediate

MEASUREMENTS

Afghan
Approx 57"/144.5cm square
Pillow
Approx 16"/40.5cm square

MATERIALS

Yarn 🔵

Bernat® *Super Value*™, 7oz/197g balls, each approx 426yd/389m (acrylic)
- 1 ball for Pillow or 3 balls for Afghan in #07407 Winter White (A)
- 1 ball in #53201 Aqua (B)
- 1 ball in #00608 Bright Yellow (C)
- 1 ball in #53417 Peony Pink (D)
- 1 ball in #53317 Lilac (D)
- 1 ball in #53009 Mushroom (E)

Hook
- Size H/8 (5mm) crochet hook, *or size needed to obtain gauge*

Notion
- 16"/40.5cm square pillow form

GAUGES

13 sc and 14 rows = 4"/10cm using size H/8 (5mm) hook.
Motif = approx 8"/20.5cm square.
TAKE TIME TO CHECK GAUGE.

MOTIF (Make 49; see chart on page 16)

Make 8 with D as Color 1, C as Color 2 and B as Color 3. Make 8 with E as Color 1, D as Color 2 and C as Color 3. Make 12 with B as Color 1, C as Color 2 and F as Color 3. Make 8 with C as Color 1, B as Color 2 and E as Color 3. Make 13 with B as Color 1, F as Color 2 and D as Color 3.

With Color 1, ch 2.

1st rnd: 8 sc in 2nd ch from hook. Join Color 2 with sl st to first sc. Break Color 1.

2nd rnd: With Color 2, ch 3 (counts as dc). 1 dc in same sp as last sl st. Ch 3. *(Yoh and draw up a loop. Yoh and draw through 2 loops on hook) twice in next st. Yoh and draw through all loops on hook—cluster made. Ch 3. Rep from * around. Join with sl st to top of ch 3. Fasten off.

3rd rnd: Join Color 3 with sl st to any ch-3 sp. Ch 4 (counts as dc and ch-1 sp). (1 dc. Ch 1) twice in same ch-3 sp. *(1 dc. Ch 1) 3 times in next ch-3 sp. Rep from * around. Join with sl st to 3rd ch of beg ch 4.

4th rnd: Sl st in first ch-1 sp. Ch 3 (counts as dc). 1 dc in same ch-1 sp. *2 dc in next ch-1 sp. Rep from * around. Join with sl st to top of ch 3.

5th rnd: Ch 1. Working in front loops only, 1 sc in same sp as last sl st. *Ch 7. Sl st in first ch of ch-7—picot made.* 1 sc in next dc. *1 sc in next dc. Picot. 1 sc in next dc. Rep from * around. Join with sl st to first sc. Fasten off.

6th rnd: Join A with sl st to any rem back loop of 5th rnd. Ch 1. Working in rem back loops of 5th rnd only, 1 sc in same sp as last sl st. *1 sc in each of next 2 sc. 1 hdc in next sc. 1 dc in next sc. 5 dc in next sc. 1 dc in next sc. 1 hdc in next sc. 1 sc in each of next 5 sc. Rep from * around, ending last rep with 1 sc in each of next 4 sc. Join with sl st to first sc.

7th rnd: Ch 2 (does not count as st). Working in both loops, 1 hdc in same sp as last sl st. *1 hdc in each of next 3 sts. 1 dc in each of next 3 sts. 5 dc in next dc. 1 dc in each of next 3 sts. 1 hdc in each of next 6 sts. Rep from * around, ending last rep with 1 hdc in each of next 5 sc. Join with sl st to first hdc.

COLORFUL COGS AFGHAN & PILLOW SET

STITCH KEY

⌒ = chain (ch)

• = slip st (sl st)

+ = single crochet (sc)

T = half double crochet (hdc)

╪ = double crochet (dc)

◊ = cluster

⌘ = picot

⌒ = worked in back loop only
⌣ = worked in front loop only

8th rnd: Ch 3 (counts as dc). 1 dc in each of next 8 sts. *5 dc in next dc. 1 dc in each of next 19 sts. Rep from * around, ending last rep with 1 dc in each of next 10 sts. Join with sl st to top of ch 3. Fasten off.

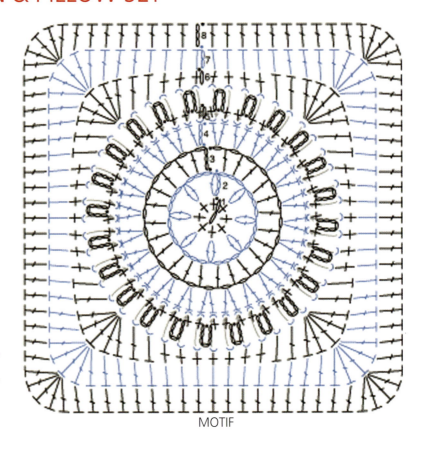

MOTIF

FINISHING
Sew Motifs tog as shown in Assembly Diagram.

Border
Join A with sl st to any corner st of Afghan. Ch 3 (counts as dc). 4 dc in same sp as sl st. 1 dc in each dc around, working 5 dc in each corner. Join with sl st to top of ch 3. Fasten off.

PILLOW

Motif (make 8 total as given for Afghan)
Make 1 with D as Color 1, C as Color 2 and B as Color 3. Make 1 with E as Color 1, D as Color 2 and C as Color 3. Make 2 with B as Color 1, C as Color 2 and F as Color 3. Make 2 with C as Color 1, B as Color 2 and E as Color 3. Make 2 with B as Color 1, F as Color 2 and D as Color 3.

FINISHING
Sew Motifs tog as shown in diagram. With WS of Front and Back tog, join A with sl st to any corner. Working through both thicknesses, work 1 sc in each sc across 3 sides of Front and Back and 3 sc in each corner sc. Insert pillow form. Crochet rem side closed. Join with sl st to first sc. Fasten off.•

AFGHAN ASSEMBLY DIAGRAM

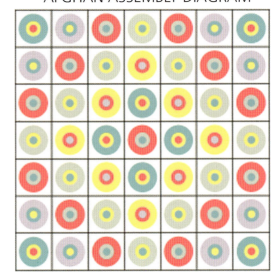

PILLOW ASSEMBLY DIAGRAM

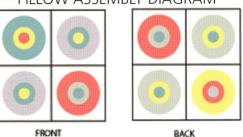

FRONT   BACK

BOUQUET BASKETS

Easy

MEASUREMENTS
Approx 5"/12.5cm in diameter x 7"/18cm tall

MATERIALS
Yarn 〔4〕
Lily® *Sugar'n Cream*®, 2½oz/71g balls, each approx 120yd/109m (cotton)
Version I
- 1 ball in #01628 Hot Orange (A)
- 1 ball in #01742 Hot Blue (B)
- 1 ball in #01740 Hot Pink (C)
- 1 ball in #01712 Hot Green (D)

Version II
- 1 ball in #01742 Hot Blue (A)
- 1 ball in #01740 Hot Pink (B)
- 1 ball in #01628 Hot Orange (C)
- 1 ball in #01712 Hot Green (D)

Version III
- 1 ball in #01740 Hot Pink (A)
- 1 ball in #01628 Hot Orange (B)
- 1 ball in #01742 Hot Blue (C)
- 1 ball in #01712 Hot Green (D)

Hook
- Sizes G/6 (4mm) and H/8 (5mm) crochet hooks, *or size needed to obtain gauge*

GAUGES
15 sc and 16 rows = 4"/10cm with size G/6 (4mm) hook.
13 sc and 14 rows = 4"/10cm with size H/8 (5mm) hook.
TAKE TIME TO CHECK GAUGE.

BASKET
With smaller hook and MC, ch 2.
1st rnd: 6 sc in 2nd ch from hook. Join with sl st to first sc.
2nd rnd: Ch 1. 2 sc in each sc around. Join with sl st to first sc. 12 sc.
3rd rnd: Ch 1. (1 sc in next sc. 2 sc in next sc) 6 times. Join with sl st to first sc. 18 sc.
4th rnd: Ch 1. (1 sc in each of next 2 sc. 2 sc in next sc) 6 times. Join with sl st to first sc. 24 sc.
5th rnd: Ch 1. (1 sc in each of next 3 sc. 2 sc in next sc) 6 times. Join with sl st to first sc. 30 sc.
6th rnd: Ch 1. 1 sc in each of next 2 sc. 2 sc in next sc. (1 sc in each of next 4 sc. 2 sc in next sc) 5 times. 1 sc in each of next 2 sc. Join with sl st to first sc. 36 sc.
7th rnd: Ch 1. (1 sc in each of next 5 sc. 2 sc in next sc) 6 times. Join with sl st to first sc. 42 sc.
8th rnd: Ch 1. 1 sc in each of next 3 sc. 2 sc in next sc. (1 sc in each of next 6 sc. 2 sc in next sc) 5 times. 1 sc in each of next 3 sc. Join with sl st to first sc. 48 sc.
9th rnd: Ch 1. (1 sc in each of next 7 sc. 2 sc in next sc) 6 times. Join with sl st to first sc. 54 sc.
10th to 14th rnds: Ch 1. 1 sc in each sc around. Join with sl st to first sc.
15th rnd: Ch 1. 1 sc in each of next 8 sc. Draw up a loop in each of next 2 sc. Yoh and draw through all loops on hook—sc2tog made. (1 sc in each of next 16 sc. Sc2tog) twice. 1 sc in each of next 8 sc. Join with sl st to first sc. 51 sc.
16th to 20th rnds: As 10th rnd.
21st rnd: Ch 1. (1 sc in each of next 15 sc. Sc2tog) 3 times. Join with sl st to first sc. 48 sts.
22nd to 24th rnds: As 10th rnd.
25th rnd: Ch 1. 1 sc in each of next 7 sc. Sc2tog. (1 sc in each of next 14 sc. Sc2tog) twice. 1 sc in each of next 7 sc. Join with sl st to first sc. 45 sc.
26th to 28th rnds: As 10th rnd.
29th rnd: Ch 1. (1 sc in each of next 13 sc. Sc2tog) 3 times. Join with sl st to first sc. 42 sts.
30th to 32nd rnds: As 10th rnd. 33rd rnd: Ch 1. 1 sc in each of next 6 sc. Sc2tog. (1 sc in each of next 12 sc. Sc2tog) twice. 1 sc in each of next 6 sc. Join with sl st to first sc. 39 sc. Ch 7 (for hanging loop). Join with sl st to first ch. Fasten off.

LARGE FLOWER (Make 1; see Chart 1 on page 56)
With larger hook and A, ch 3. Join with sl st in first ch to form a ring.
1st rnd: Ch 1. 7 sc into ring. Join with sl st to first sc.

2nd rnd: Ch 1. 1 sc in first sc. Ch 10. 3 sc in 2nd ch from hook. 3 sc in each of next 8 ch. *1 sc in next sc. Ch 10. 3 sc in 2nd ch from hook. 3 sc in each of next 8 ch. Rep from * 5 times more. Join with sl st to first sc. Fasten off. 7 petals.

SMALL FLOWER (Make 1; see Chart 2 on page 56)

With larger hook and B, ch 2.

1st rnd: 5 sc in 2nd ch from hook. Join with sl st to first sc.

2nd rnd: Ch 1. 1 sc in first sc. Ch 7. 3 sc in 2nd ch from hook. 3 sc in each of next 5 ch. *1 sc in next sc. Ch 7. 3 sc in 2nd ch from hook. 3 sc in each of next 5 ch. Rep from * 3 times more. Join with sl st to first sc. Fasten off. 5 petals.

LEAF (Make 4)

With larger hook and C, ch 5.

1st rnd: 1 sc in 2nd ch from hook. 1 hdc in next ch. 1 dc in next ch. (2 hdc.

Ch 2. Sl st in 2nd ch from hook. 2 hdc) in last ch. Working into opposite side of ch, work 1 dc in next ch. 1 hdc in next ch. 1 sc in last ch. Join with sl st to first sc. Fasten off, leaving a long tail for stitching.

FINISHING

Fold top edge approx 2½"/6cm to RS. Layer Small Flower on top of Large Flower and sew on button to center through all layers. Sew Flower to Basket front as shown in picture. Sew Leaves randomly around Flowers as shown in picture.•

BRIGHT SQUARES BLANKET & PILLOW

Easy

MEASUREMENTS
Blanket
Approx 48"/122cm x 57"/144.5cm
Pillow
Approx 18"/45.5cm square

MATERIALS
Yarn
Patons® *Canadiana*™, 3½oz/100g balls, each approx 205yd/187m (acrylic)
For Blanket or Pillow
- 1 ball in #10744 Medium Teal (A)
- 1 ball in #10610 Fool's Gold (B)
- 1 ball in #10628 Tangy (C)
- 1 ball in #10008 Aran (D)
- 1 ball in #10010 Flax (E)
- 1 ball in #10630 Burnt Orange (F)
- 1 ball in #10013 Timber (G)
- 1 ball in #10712 Lime Juice (H)
- 1 ball in #10745 Dark Teal (I)

Hook
- Size H/8 (5mm) crochet hook, *or size needed to obtain gauge*

Notion
- 18"/45.5cm square pillow form

GAUGE
15 dc and 7 rows = 4"/10cm using size H/8 (5mm) hook.
TAKE TIME TO CHECK GAUGE.

BLANKET
Large Motif
With Color 1, ch 5. Join with sl st in first ch to form a ring.
1st rnd: Ch 3 (counts as dc). [3 dc. (Ch 3. 4 dc) 3 times] all in ring. Ch 3. Join with sl st to top of ch 3. Fasten off.
2nd rnd: Join Color 2 with sl st in any ch-3 sp. Ch 3 (counts as dc). (1 dc. Ch 3. 2 dc) in same sp as sl st. *1 dc in each dc across to next ch-3 sp. (2 dc. Ch 3. 2 dc) in next ch-3 sp. Rep from * twice more. 1 dc in each dc to end of rnd. Join with sl st to top of ch 3. Fasten off.
3rd rnd: Join Color 3 with sl st in any ch-3 sp. As 2nd rnd. Fasten off.
4th rnd: Join Color 4 with sl st in any ch-3 sp. As 2nd rnd. Fasten off.
5th rnd: Join Color 5 with sl st in any ch-3 sp. As 2nd rnd. Do not fasten off.
6th rnd: Ch 3 (counts as dc). 1 dc in next dc. *(2 dc. Ch 3. 2 dc) in next ch-3 sp. 1 dc in each dc across to next ch-3 sp. Rep from * twice more. (2 dc. Ch 3. 2 dc) in next ch-3 sp. 1 dc in each dc to end of rnd. Join with sl st to top of ch 3. Fasten off.
7th rnd: Join Color 6 with sl st in any ch-3 sp. As 2nd rnd. Fasten off.

Small Motif
With Color 1, ch 5. Join with sl st in first ch to form a ring.
1st rnd: Ch 3 (counts as dc). [3 dc. (Ch 3. 4 dc) 3 times] all in ring. Ch 3. Join with sl st to top of ch 3. Fasten off.
2nd rnd: Join Color 2 with sl st in any ch-3 sp. Ch 3 (counts as dc). (1 dc. Ch 3. 2 dc) in same sp as sl st. *1 dc in each dc across to next ch-3 sp. (2 dc. Ch 3. 2 dc) in next ch-3 sp. Rep from * twice more. 1 dc in each dc to end of rnd. Join with sl st to top of ch 3. Fasten off.
3rd rnd: Join Color 3 with sl st in any ch-3 sp. As 2nd rnd. Fasten off.

FINISHING
Sew Motifs tog following Diagram I (see page 22).

Edging

1st rnd: With RS facing, join A with sl st in bottom right corner. Ch 1. Work sc evenly around outer edge of Blanket having 3 sc in each corner. Join B with sl st in first sc.
2nd rnd: With B, ch 1. Work 1 sc in each sc around, having 3 sc in each corner sc. Join C with sl st in first sc.
3rd rnd: With C, as 2nd rnd, joining D at end of rnd.
4th rnd: With D, as 2nd rnd, joining G at end of rnd.
5th rnd: With G, as 2nd rnd. Fasten off.

PILLOW

Make Large and Small Motifs as given for Blanket, following Guides on page 22 for colors and quantities of Large and Small Motifs.

FINISHING

Sew Motifs tog following Diagram II (see page 22) shown for each Front and Back piece.

BRIGHT SQUARES BLANKET & PILLOW

Edging

1st rnd: With WS facing each other, place Front and Back pieces tog. With RS of Front facing, join A through both thicknesses at bottom right corner and work 1 row of sc through both thicknesses to join pieces, working 3 sc in corners. *Do not* work across bottom edge. Insert pillow form. Complete working sc across bottom edge. Join B with sl st to first sc. Fasten off. •

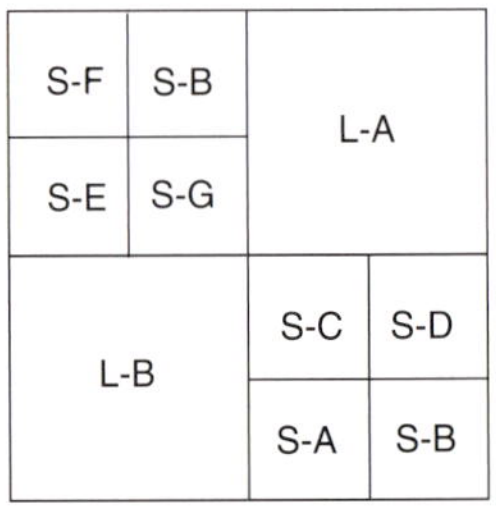

LARGE MOTIFS GUIDE

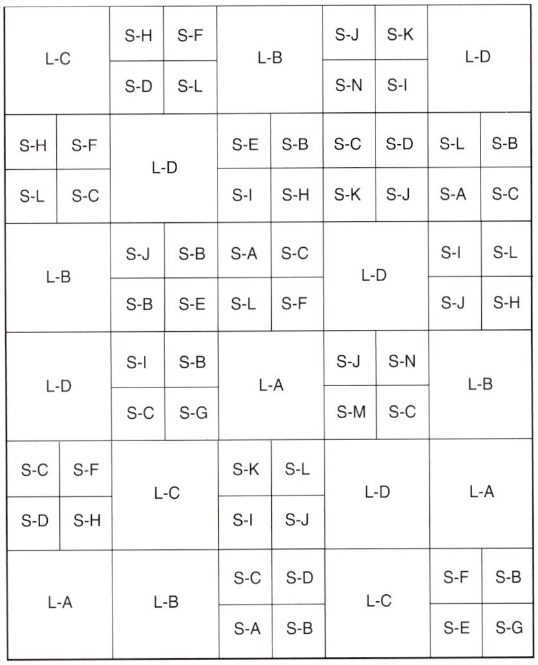

Name	(Make)	Color 1	Color 2	Color 3	Color 4	Color 5	Color 6
L-A	3	D	H	I	A	C	G
L-B	4	F	E	D	B	H	A
L-C	3	C	F	G	I	A	C
L-D	5	H	B	E	C	D	F

SMALL MOTIFS GUIDE

Name	(Make)	Color 1	Color 2	Color 3
S-A	3	G	E	F
S-B	7	B	C	I
S-C	8	C	D	G
S-D	4	D	H	A
S-E	3	H	A	G
S-F	5	I	E	H
S-G	2	F	G	A
S-H	5	A	G	F
S-I	5	B	E	H
S-J	6	E	B	C
S-K	3	C	B	H
S-L	6	H	A	B
S-M	1	H	I	A
S-N	2	G	E	I

LARGE MOTIFS GUIDE

Name	(Make)	Color 1	Color 2	Color 3	Color 4	Color 5	Color 6
L-A	2	D	H	I	A	C	G
L-B	2	F	E	D	B	H	A

SMALL MOTIFS GUIDE

Name	(Make)	Color 1	Color 2	Color 3
S-A	2	G	E	F
S-B	4	B	C	I
S-C	2	C	D	G
S-D	2	D	H	A
S-E	2	H	A	G
S-F	2	I	E	H
S-G	2	F	G	A

Diagram I

Diagram II

COTTON DISHCLOTH

Beginner

MEASUREMENTS
Approx 9"/23cm square

MATERIALS
Yarn (4)

Lily® *Sugar'n Cream*® *Solids*, 2½oz/71g balls, each approx 120yd/109m (cotton), or *Sugar'n Cream*® *Ombres*, 2oz/57g balls, each 95yd/86m (cotton)
• 1 ball in #01712 Hot Green or #01628 Hot Orange or #02743 Summer Splash or #02741 Playtime

Hook
• Size I/9 (5.5mm) crochet hook, *or size needed to obtain gauge*

GAUGE
14 sts and 14 rows = 4"/10cm using size I/9 (5.5mm) in pat.
TAKE TIME TO CHECK GAUGE.

DISHCLOTH
Ch 32.

1st row: (RS) 1 sc in 2nd ch from hook. *Ch 1. Miss next ch. 1 sc in next ch. Rep from * to end of ch. Turn. 31 sts.

2nd row: Ch 1. 1 sc in first sc. 1 sc in next ch-1 sp. *Ch 1. Miss next sc. 1 sc in next ch-1 sp. Rep from * to last sc. 1 sc in last sc. Turn.

3rd row: Ch 1. 1 sc in first sc. *Ch 1. Miss next sc. 1 sc in next ch-1 sp. Rep from * to last 2 sc. Ch 1. Miss next sc. 1 sc in last sc. Turn.

Rep last 2 rows until work from beg measures 9"/23cm, ending with RS facing for next row. Ch 8. Sl st in top of last sc (loop). Fasten off.•

CITRUS SLICE RUG

Easy

MEASUREMENTS
Approx 28"/71cm long x 14"/35.5cm wide

MATERIALS
Yarn (4)
Lily® *Sugar'n Cream*®, 2½oz/71g balls, each approx 120yd/109m (cotton)
- 6 balls in #01628 Hot Orange (A)
- 2 balls in #00001 White (B)

Hook
- Size P/Q-19 (15mm) crochet hook, *or size needed to obtain gauge*

Notions
- 3 stitch markers

GAUGE
5 dc and 3 rows = 4"/10cm using size P/Q-19 (15mm) hook with 6 strands of yarn held together.
TAKE TIME TO CHECK GAUGE.

NOTES
- Rug is worked holding 6 strands of yarn tog throughout. For ease of working, wind Contrast B into 6 equal balls.
- Ch 3 at beg of row counts as dc.

RUG
With 6 strands of A held tog, ch 4.

1st row: (RS) 5 dc in 4th ch from hook (turning ch 3 counts as dc). Turn. 6 dc.

2nd row: Ch 3. 1 dc in first dc. 2 dc in each dc to end of row. Turn. 12 dc.

3rd row: Ch 3. 1 dc in first dc. *1 dc in next dc. 2 dc in next dc. Rep from * to last dc. 1 dc in last dc. Turn. 18 dc.

4th row: Ch 3. 1 dc in first dc. *1 dc in each of next 2 dc. 2 dc in next dc. Rep from * to last 2 dc. 1 dc in each of last 2 dc. Turn. 24 dc.

5th row: Ch 3. 1 dc in first dc. *1 dc in each of next 3 dc. 2 dc in next dc. Rep from * to last 3 dc. 1 dc in each of last 3 dc. Turn. 30 dc.

6th row: Ch 3. 1 dc in first dc. *1 dc in each of next 4 dc. 2 dc in next dc. Rep from * to last 4 dc. 1 dc in each of last 4 dc. Turn. 36 dc.

7th row: Ch 3. 1 dc in first dc. *1 dc in each of next 5 dc. 2 dc in next dc. Rep from * to last 5 dc. 1 dc in each of last 5 dc. Turn. 42 dc.

8th row: Ch 3. 1 dc in first dc. *1 dc in each of next 6 dc. 2 dc in next dc. Rep from * to last 6 dc. 1 dc in each of last 6 dc. Do not break A. Join B. Turn. 48 dc.

9th row: (RS) With B, ch 2 (does not count as hdc). 2 hdc in same st as last sl st. *1 hdc in each of next 7 dc. 2 hdc in next dc. Rep from * to last 7 dc. 1 hdc in each of last 7 dc. 54 hdc. Fasten off B. Do not turn.

10th row: (RS) Return A to hook, sl st in first hdc. Ch 3 (counts as dc). 1 dc in first hdc. *1 dc in each of next 8 hdc. 2 dc in next hdc. Rep from * to last 8 hdc. 1 dc in each of last 8 hdc. 60 dc. Fasten off.

Orange Sections
Place markers as follows: On 8th row at center of Rug, then at the halfway mark between center and bottom edge of Rug (see photo below and diagram on page 56). With 3 strands of B held tog and RS facing, sl st in same ch from 1st row where 5 dc were worked. Working in a straight line to center marker and keeping working yarn at WS, sl st in each row to marker, being sure to keep sl sts loose. Rep for rem sections.

FINISHING
With 6 strands of B held tog and RS facing, join with sl st to top of last dc of 10th row. Ch 1. Work 1 row of sc along straight bottom edge. Fasten off.•

GINGHAM PICNIC BLANKET

Easy

MEASUREMENTS
Approx 38"/96.5cm square

MATERIALS

Yarn

Caron® *Simply Soft®*, 6oz/170g balls, each approx 315yd/288m (acrylic)
- 3 balls #9701 White (A)
- 3 balls #9712 Soft Blue (B)
- 2 balls #9767 Royal Blue (C)

Hook
- Size I/9 (5.5mm) crochet hook, *or size needed to obtain gauge*

GAUGE
14 sc and 15 rows = 4"/10cm using size I/9 (5.5m) hook.
TAKE TIME TO CHECK GAUGE.

NOTES
- To change colors, work to last 2 loops on hook of first color. Draw new color through last 2 loops and proceed with new color.
- Carry yarn not in use loosely across top of previous row and work sts around it to prevent stranding.

BLANKET
With A, ch 126. Foundation ch worked over a multiple of 10 ch plus 6.

1st row: With A, 1 sc in 2nd ch from hook and each of next 4 ch. *With B, 1 sc in each of next 5 ch. With A, 1 sc in each of next 5 ch. Rep from * to end of chain. Turn. 125 sc.

2nd to 5th rows: With A, ch 1. 1 sc in each of first 5 sc. *With B, 1 sc in each of next 5 sc. With A, 1 sc in each of next 5 sc. Rep from * to end of row. Turn. Break A at end of last row.

6th to 10th rows: With B, ch 1. 1 sc in each of first 5 sc. *With C, 1 sc in each of next 5 sc. With B, 1 sc in each of next 5 sc. Rep from * to end of row. Turn. Break C at end of last row.

11th row: As 2nd row.

Rep 2nd to 11th rows for Gingham Pat until work from beg measures approx 36"/91.5cm, ending on 5th row of pat. Do not break A.

Final row: As 2nd row. Fasten off.

FINISHING

Border

1st rnd: (RS) Join A with sl st to any corner. Ch 1. 2 sc in same sp as sl st. Work in sc around, having 3 sc in each corner. 1 sc in same sp as first 2 sc. Join with sl st to first sc.

2nd rnd: Ch 1. 2 sc in same sp as last sl st. 1 sc in each sc around, having 3 sc in each corner sc. 1 sc in same sp as first 2 sc. Join with sl st to first sc.

3rd and 4th rnds: Rep last rnd twice more. Fasten off.•

HANDY BASKET

Easy

MEASUREMENTS
Approx 10"/25.5cm in diameter x 12"/30.5cm tall

MATERIALS
Yarn
Lily® *Sugar'n Cream*®, 2½oz/71g balls, each approx 120yd/109m (cotton)
- 6 balls in #01004 Soft Ecru (A)
- 2 balls in #01131 Dazzle Blue (B)

Hook
- Size 7 (4.5mm) crochet hook, *or size needed to obtain gauge*

Notions
- Stitch marker

GAUGE
12 sc and 13 rows = 4"/10cm using size 7 (4.5mm) hook and holding 2 strands of yarn together.
TAKE TIME TO CHECK GAUGE.

BASKET
Base
With 2 strands of A, ch 2.
1st rnd: 6 sc in 2nd ch from hook. Join with sl st to first sc.
2nd rnd: Ch 1. 2 sc in each sc around. Join with sl st to first sc. 12 sc.
3rd rnd: Ch 1. 2 sc in same sc as last sl st. 1 sc in next sc. *2 sc in next sc. 1 sc in next sc. Rep from * around. Join with sl st to first sc. 18 sc.
4th rnd: Ch 1. 2 sc in same sc as last sl st. 1 sc in each of next 2 sc. *2 sc in next sc. 1 sc in each of next 2 sc. Rep from * around. Join with sl st to first sc. 24 sc.
5th rnd: Ch 1. 2 sc in same sc as last sl st. 1 sc in each of next 3 sc. *2 sc in next sc. 1 sc in each of next 3 sc. Rep from * around. Join with sl st to first sc. 30 sc.
6th rnd: Ch 1. 2 sc in same sc as last sl st. 1 sc in each of next 4 sc. *2 sc in next sc. 1 sc in each of next 4 sc. Rep from * around. Join with sl st to first sc. 36 sc.

7th to 15th rnds: Cont in this manner, inc 6 sc evenly around each rnd. 90 sc.
16th rnd: Ch 1. 1 sc in each sc around. Join with sl st in first sc.
17th rnd: Ch 1. Working in back loops only, *2 sc in same sp as last sl st. 1 sc in each of next 21 sc. Rep from * around to last 2 sc. 1 sc in each of last 2 sc. Join with sl st to first sc. 94 sc. Place marker at end of last rnd.

Main Section
Next rnd: Ch 2 (does not counts as hdc). 1 hdc in same sp as last sl st. 1 hdc in each sc around. Join with sl st to first hdc.
Next rnd: Ch 2 (does not count as hdc). *1 hdc in sp between next 2 hdc. Rep from * around, ending with 1 hdc in sp between last hdc and first hdc of rnd. Join with sl st to first hdc. 94 hdc.
Rep last rnd until work from marked rnd measures 9½"/24.5cm. Join 2 strands of B at end of last rnd. Break A.
With 2 strands of B, rep last rnd 3 times more.

Make Handles
Next rnd: Ch 2 (does not count as hdc). (1 hdc in sp between next 2 hdc) 6 times. *Ch 18. Skip next 18 sps between 2 hdc.* (1 hdc in sp between next 2 hdc) 29 times. Rep from * to * once more. **1 hdc in sp between next 2 hdc. Rep from ** around, ending with 1 hdc in sp between last hdc and first hdc of rnd. Join with sl st to first hdc.
Next rnd: Ch 2 (does not count as hdc). (1 hdc in sp between next 2 hdc) 6 times. Work 18 hdc in next ch-18 sp. (1 hdc in sp between next 2 hdc) 29 times. Work 18 hdc in next ch-18 sp. *1 hdc in sp between next 2 hdc. Rep from * around, ending with 1 hdc in sp between last hdc and first hdc of rnd. Join with sl st to first hdc. 94 hdc.
Next rnd: Ch 2 (does not count as hdc). *1 hdc in sp between next 2 hdc. Rep from * around, ending with 1 hdc in sp between last hdc and first hdc of rnd. Join with sl st to first hdc. Fasten off.●

FULL CIRCLE PILLOW

Easy

MEASUREMENTS
Approx 14"/35.5cm diameter

MATERIALS
Yarn
Caron® *Simply Soft*® or *Simply Soft*® *Brites*™, 6oz/170g balls, each approx 315yd/288m (acrylic)
• 2 balls in #9759 Ocean *Simply Soft*® or #B9608 Blue Mint or #B9605 Mango *Simply Soft*® *Brites*™

Hook
• Size 7 (4.5mm) crochet hook, *or size needed to obtain gauge*

Notions
• Stitch marker
• Round pillow form 14"/35.5cm diameter

GAUGE
14 dc and 7 rows = 4"/10cm using size 7 (4.5mm) hook.
TAKE TIME TO CHECK GAUGE.

STITCH GLOSSARY
Dc2tog = (Yoh and draw up a loop in next stitch. Yoh and draw through 2 loops on hook) twice. Yoh and draw through all loops on hook.

NOTES
• Ch 3 at beg of rnd counts as dc throughout.
• Pillow is worked in one piece.

PILLOW
Ch 4.
1st rnd: 17 dc in 4th ch from hook. Join with sl st to top of ch-3. 18 dc.
2nd rnd: Ch 3. 1 dc in same sp as last sl st. 1 dc in next dc. *2 dc in next dc. 1 dc in next dc. Rep from * around. Join with sl st to top of ch-3. 27 dc.
3rd rnd: Ch 3. (2 dc in next dc. 1 dc in each of next 2 dc) 8 times. 2 dc in next dc. 1 dc in last dc. Join with sl st to top of ch-3. 36 dc.
4th rnd: Ch 3. 1 dc in each of next 2 dc. (2 dc in next dc. 1 dc in each of next 3 dc) 8 times. 2 dc in next dc. Join with sl st to top of ch-3. 45 dc.
5th rnd: Ch 3. (2 dc in next dc. 1 dc in each of next 4 dc) 8 times. 2 dc in next dc. 1 dc in each of next 3 dc. Join with sl st to top of ch-3. 54 dc.
6th rnd: Ch 3. 1 dc in each of next 4 dc. (2 dc in next dc. 1 dc in each of next 5 dc) 8 times. 2 dc in last dc. Join with sl st to top of ch-3. 63 dc.
7th rnd: Ch 3. (2 dc in next dc. 1 dc in each of next 6 dc) 8 times. 2 dc in next dc. 1 dc in each of last 5 dc. Join with sl st to top of ch-3. 72 dc.
8th rnd: Ch 3. 1 dc in each of next 6 dc. (2 dc in next dc. 1 dc in each of next 7 dc) 8 times. 2 dc in last dc. Join with sl st to top of ch-3. 81 dc.
Cont in same manner, inc 9 dc every rnd until there are 153 dc. Place marker at end of rnd.
Next 3 rnds: Ch 3. 1 dc in each dc around. Join with sl st to top of ch-3.

Proceed as follows:
1st rnd: Ch 3. 1 dc in each of next 14 dc. Dc2tog. (1 dc in each of next 15 dc. Dc2tog) 8 times. Join with sl st to top of ch-3. 144 sts rem.
2nd rnd: Ch 3. 1 dc in each of next 13 dc. Dc2tog. (1 dc in each of next 14 dc. Dc2tog) 8 times. Join with sl st to top of ch-3. 135 sts rem.
3rd rnd: Ch 3. 1 dc in each of next 12 dc. Dc2tog. (1 dc in each of next 13 dc. Dc2tog) 8 times. Join with sl st to top of ch-3. 126 sts rem.
4th rnd: Ch 3. 1 dc in each of next 11 dc. Dc2tog. (1 dc in each of next 12 dc. Dc2tog) 8 times. Join with sl st to top of ch-3. 117 sts rem. Insert pillow form. Cont in same manner, dec 9 dc every rnd until 18 sts rem. Fasten off, leaving a long end. Thread end through rem sts. Pull tightly and fasten securely.•

FLOWER POWER TABLE RUNNER

Easy

MEASUREMENTS
Approx 13"/33cm wide x 65"/165cm long

MATERIALS
Yarn 4

Lily® *Sugar'n Cream*®, 2½oz/71g balls, each approx 120yd/109m (cotton)
- 1 ball in #00082 Jute (A)
- 1 ball in #00004 Ecru (B)
- 1 ball in #01322 Lilac (C)
- 1 ball in #01530 Country Red (D)
- 1 ball in #01201 Seabreeze (E)
- 1 ball in #01699 Tangerine (F)
- 1 ball in #01612 Country Yellow (G)
- 1 ball in #01712 Hot Green (H)

Hook
- Size H/8 (5mm) crochet hook, *or size needed to obtain gauge*

GAUGE
13 sc and 14 rows = 4"/10cm using size H/8 (5mm) hook. *TAKE TIME TO CHECK GAUGE.*

TABLE RUNNER
Note: See Chart on page 34 and Assembly Diagram on page 56..

First Flower
**With Color 1, ch 2.
1st rnd: 12 sc in 2nd ch from hook. Join with sl st to first sc.
2nd rnd: Ch 6 (counts as 1 dc. Ch 3). Skip next sc. *1 dc in next sc. Ch 3. Skip next sc. Rep from * around. Join with sl st to 3rd ch of beg ch-6. Fasten off.
3rd rnd: Join Color 2 with sl st to any ch-3 sp. Ch 3. 4 dc in same ch-3 sp as last sl st. *Ch 4. 5 dc in next ch-3 sp. Rep from * around. Ch 4. Join with sl st to top of beg ch 3.**

4th rnd: Sl st in each of next 2 dc. Ch 1. 1 sc in same sp as last sl st. *Ch 1 Skip next 2 dc. [(1 dc. Ch 1) twice. 1 dc. Ch 3. (1 dc. Ch 1) 3 times] all in next ch-4 sp. Skip next 2 dc. 1 sc in next sc. Rep from * around. Join with sl st to first sc. Fasten off.

Join Second Flower
Work from ** to ** as given for First Flower.
4th rnd: Sl st in each of next 2 dc. Ch 1. 1 sc in same sp as last sl st. Ch 1. Skip next 2 dc. [(1 dc. Ch 1) twice. 1 dc. Ch 1. Sl st corresponding ch-3 sp of adjoining Motif (First Flower). Ch 1. (1 dc. Ch 1) 3 times] all in next ch-4 sp. *Ch 1. Skip next 2 dc. 1 sc in next dc. Skip next 2 dc. Ch 1. [(1 dc. Ch 1) twice. 1 dc. Ch 3. (1 dc. Ch 1) 3 times] all in next ch-4 sp. Rep from * around. Join with sl st to first sc. Fasten off.

Join Third Flower
Work from ** to ** as given for First Flower.
4th rnd: Sl st in each of next 2 dc. Ch 1. 1 sc in same sp as last sl st. *Ch 1. Skip next 2 dc. [(1 dc. Ch 1) twice. 1 dc. Ch 1. Sl st in corresponding ch-3 sp of adjoining Flower (First Flower) Ch 1. (1 dc. Ch 1) 3 times] all in next ch-4 sp. Ch 1. Skip next 2 dc. 1 sc in next dc. Rep from * once more. *Ch 1. Skip next 2 dc. [(1 dc. Ch 1) twice. 1 dc. (1 dc. Ch 1) 3 times] all in next ch-4 sp. Rep from * around. Join with sl st to first sc. Fasten off.

Join Fourth Flower
Work from ** to ** as given for First Flower.
4th rnd: Sl st in each of next 2 dc. Ch 1. 1 sc in same sp as last sl st. *Ch 1. Skip next 2 dc. [(1 dc. Ch 1) twice. 1 dc. Ch 1. Sl st in corresponding ch-3 sp of adjoining Motif (Third Flower). Ch 1. (1 dc. Ch 1) 3 times] all in next ch-4 sp. Ch 1. Skip next 2 dc. 1 sc in next dc. Rep from * twice more (Joining to Second Flower).

FLOWER POWER TABLE RUNNER

Ch 1. Skip next 2 dc. [(1 dc. Ch 1) twice. 1 dc. (1 dc. Ch 1) 3 times] all in next ch-4 sp. Rep from * around. Join with sl st to first sc. Fasten off.

Cont as established for Third and Fourth Flowers, in the following color sequence:
Motif A: A as Color 1. E as Color 2.
Motif B: B as Color 1. C as Color 2.
Motif C: B as Color 1. D as Color 2.
Motif D: A as Color 1. F as Color 2.
Motif E: F as Color 1. G as Color 2.

Center Joining Motif
With H, ch 2.

1st rnd: 4 sc in 2nd ch from hook. Join with sl st to first sc. 4 sc.
2nd rnd: Ch 4. *[Yoh twice and draw up a loop. (Yoh and draw through 2 loops on hook) twice] 3 times in same sc as last sl st. Yoh and draw through 4 loops on hook—beg cluster made.
Ch 8. *[Yoh twice and draw up a loop. (Yoh and draw through 2 loops on hook) twice] 4 times in next sc. Yoh and draw through 5 loops on hook. Ch 8. Rep from * twice more. Join with sl st to top of Beg cluster.
3rd rnd: Sl st in first ch-8 sp. Ch 1. 1 sc in same sp as last sl st. *Ch 3. Sl st in corresponding sc of adjoining Flower. Ch 3. 1 sc in same ch-8 sp as last sc. Ch 4. Sl st in corresponding sl st of adjoining Flowers. Ch 4. 1 sc in next ch-8 sp. Rep from * around. Join with sl st to first sc. Fasten off.•

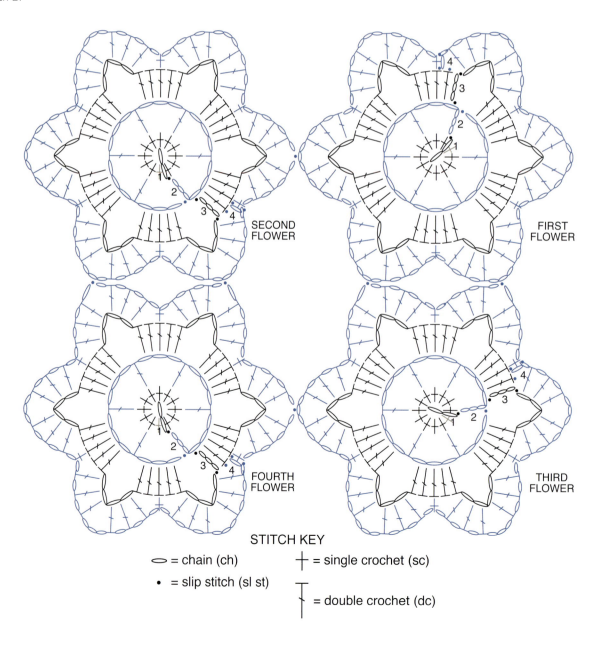

STITCH KEY

◦ = chain (ch)
• = slip stitch (sl st)
+ = single crochet (sc)
⊤ = double crochet (dc)

COLOR WHEEL PILLOW

Easy

MEASUREMENTS
Approx 16"/40.5cm diameter

MATERIALS
Yarn
Caron® Simply Soft®, 6oz/170g balls, each approx 315yd/288m (acrylic)
- 1 ball in #9762 Burgundy (A)
- 1 ball in #9763 Harvest Red (B)
- 1 ball in #B9604 Watermelon (C)
- 1 ball in #B9605 Mango (D)
- 1 ball in #9778 Orange (E)
- 1 ball in #9782 Gold (F)
- 1 ball in #9771 Chartreuse (G)
- 1 ball in #9779 Green (H)

Hook
- Size 7 (4.5mm) crochet hook, *or size needed to obtain gauge*

Notion
- Round pillow form 16"/40.5cm diameter

GAUGE
14 sc and 16 rows = 4"/10cm using size 7 (4.5mm) hook.
TAKE TIME TO CHECK GAUGE.

NOTES
- Ch 3 at beg of rnd counts as dc throughout.
- To join new color, work to last 2 loops on hook. Draw new color through last 2 loops then proceed with new color.

FRONT and BACK (Make alike)
With A, ch 4.
1st rnd: 15 dc in 4th ch from hook. Join with sl st to top of ch 3. 16 dc.
2nd rnd: Ch 3. 1 dc in same sp as last sl st. 2 dc in each dc around. Join B with sl st to top of ch 3. 32 dc.
3rd rnd: With B, ch 1. 1 sc in each dc around. Join with sl st to first sc.
4th rnd: Ch 3. 1 dc in same sp as last sl st. 1 dc in next sc. (2 dc in next sc. 1 dc in next sc) 15 times. Join C with sl st to top of ch 3. 48 dc.
5th rnd: With C, as 3rd rnd.
6th rnd: Ch 3. 1 dc in next sc. 2 dc in next sc. (1 dc in each of next 2 sc. 2 dc in next sc) 15 times. Join D with sl st to top of ch 3. 64 dc.
7th rnd: With D, as 3rd rnd.
8th rnd: Ch 3. 1 dc in same sp as last sl st. 1 dc in each of next 3 sc. (2 dc in next sc. 1 dc in each of next 3 sc) 15 times. Join E with sl st to top of ch 3. 80 dc.
9th rnd: With E, as 3rd rnd.
10th rnd: Ch 3. 1 dc in each of next 3 sc. 2 dc in next sc. (1 dc in each of next 4 sc. 2 dc in next sc) 15 times. Join F with sl st to top of ch 3. 96 dc.
11th rnd: With F, as 3rd rnd.
12th rnd: Ch 3. 1 dc in same sp as last sl st. 1 dc in each of next 5 sc. (2 dc in next sc. 1 dc in each of next 5 sc) 15 times. Join G with sl st to top of ch 3. 112 dc.
13th rnd: With G, as 3rd rnd.
14th rnd: Ch 3. 1 dc in each of next 5 sc. 2 dc in next sc. (1 dc in each of next 6 sc. 2 dc in next sc) 15 times. Join H with sl st to top of ch 3. 128 dc.
15th rnd: With H, as 3rd rnd.
16th rnd: Ch 3. 1 dc in each sc around. Join with sl st to top of ch 3. Fasten off.
Note: Insert pillow form at half-way point of joining Front and Back.

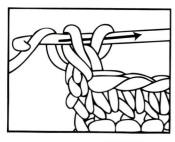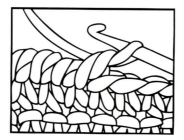
REVERSE SINGLE CROCHET

Join Front and Back

1st rnd: With WS facing each other, join H with sl st to any dc. Working through both thicknesses, work 1 sc in each dc around. Join with sl st to first sc.

2nd rnd: Working from left to right instead of from right to left, work 1 reverse sc in each sc around. Join with sl st to first sc. Fasten off.•

HOT HIBISCUS TEA COZY

Intermediate

SIZE
To fit a 4-cup (6-cup) teapot

MATERIALS
Yarn (4)
Lily® *Sugar'n Cream*®, 2½oz/71g balls, each approx 120yd/109m (cotton)
- 1 ball in #01740 Hot Pink (A)
- 1 ball in #01317 Hot Purple (B)
- 1 ball in #01742 Hot Blue (C)
- 1 ball in #01712 Hot Green (D)
- 1 ball in #01628 Hot Orange (F)
- 1 ball in #00095 Red (G)

Yarn (4)
Lily® *Sugar'n Cream*® Scents, 2oz/56.7g balls, each 95yd/86m (cotton)
- 1 ball in #24003 Vanilla Bouquet (E)

Hook
- Size H/8 (5mm) crochet hook, *or size needed to obtain gauge*

GAUGE
13 sc and 14 rows = 4"/10cm using size H/8 (5mm) hook.
TAKE TIME TO CHECK GAUGE.

NOTE
- The instructions are written for smallest size. If changes are necessary for larger size, the instructions will be written thus ( ).

COZY (Front and Back—make alike)
Stripe Pat
Work 2 rows of each color in the following sequence: A, B, C, D, E, F, G, F, E, D, C, B, A. (See Chart 1 on page 40).
With A, ch 29 (36).

1st row: (RS) 1 sc in 2nd ch from hook. 1 sc in each of next 2 ch. [Ch 10 (loop). Skip next ch. 1 sc in each of next 6 ch] 3 (4) times. Ch 10 (loop). Skip next ch. 1 sc in each of next 3 ch. Turn.

2nd row: Ch 1. 1 sc in each of next 3 sc. [Ch 10 (loop). Skip next ch-10 sp. 1 sc in each of next 6 sc] 3 (4) times. Ch 10 (loop). Skip next ch-10 sp. 1 sc in each of next 3 sc. Turn. First 2 rows of Stripe Pat are complete. Keeping cont of Stripe Pat, rep last row until work from beg measures approx 4 (5)"/10 (12.5)cm, ending with a WS row.

Shape Top (See Chart 2 on page 40).
1st row: Ch 1. 1 sc in each of next 3 sc. [Ch 10 (loop). Skip next ch-10 sp. 1 sc in each of next 2 sc. Draw up a loop in each of next 2 sc. Yoh and draw through all loops on hook—sc2tog made. 1 sc in each of next 2 sc] 3 (4) times. Ch 10 (loop). Skip next ch-10 sp. 1 sc in each of next 3 sc. Turn.

2nd row: Ch 1. 1 sc in first sc. Sc2tog. [Ch 10 (loop). Skip next ch-10 sp. 1 sc in each of next 2 sc. Sc2tog. 1 sc in next sc] 3 (4) times. Ch 10 (loop). Skip next ch-10 sp. Sc2tog. 1 sc in last sc. Turn.

3rd row: Ch 1. 1 sc in each of first 2 sc. [Ch 10 (loop). Skip next ch-10 sp. 1 sc in each of next 4 sc] 3 (4) times. Ch 10 (loop). Skip next ch-10 sp. 1 sc in each of last 2 sc. Turn.

4th row: Ch 1. 1 sc in each of first 2 sc. [Ch 10 (loop). Skip next ch-10 sp. 1 sc in next sc. Sc2tog. 1 sc in next sc] 3 (4) times. Ch 10 (loop). Skip next ch-10 sp. 1 sc in each of last 2 sc. Turn.

5th row: Ch 1. 1 sc in each of first 2 sc. [Ch 10 (loop). Skip next ch-10 sp. 1 sc in each of next 3 sts] 3 (4) times. Ch 10 (loop). Skip next ch-10 sp. 1 sc in each of last 2 sc. Turn.

HOT HIBISCUS TEA COZY

6th row: Ch 1. Sc2tog. [Ch 10 (loop). Skip next ch-10 sp. Draw up a loop in each of next 3 sc. Yoh and draw through all loops on hook—sc3tog made] 3 (4) times. Ch 10 (loop). Skip next ch-10 sp. Sc2tog. Turn.

Chaining Loops (See Chart 3).
Pick up ch-10 loops from 3rd and 4th rows and pull tog through ch-10 loops from 1st and 2nd rows. Pick up ch-10 loops from 5th and 6th rows and pull tog through ch-10 loops from 3rd and 4th rows. Pick up ch-10 loops from 7th and 8th rows and pull tog through ch-10 loops from 5th and 6th rows. Rep in same manner for all ch-10 loops as shown in picture.
Next row: Ch 1. 1 sc in first st. (2 sc in 2 ch-10 loops formed after chaining. 1 sc in next st) 4 (5) times. 1 sc in last sc. Turn. 11 (14) sc. Next row: Ch 1. 1 sc in first sc. (Sc2tog) 5 (7) times. 1 sc in next 1 (0) sc. Fasten off. Sew seams 2½ (3¼)"/6 (8.5)cm in from top and bottom edges for spout and handle openings.

Flower (See Chart 4).
With D, ch 5. Join with sl st to first ch to form a ring.
1st rnd: Ch 1. 10 sc in ring. Join with sl st to first sc.
2nd rnd: Working into front loops only, ch 1. 1 sc in same sp as sl st. Ch 3. Sl st in top of last sc—picot made. *1 sc in next sc. Picot. Rep from * around. Join with sl st to first sc. Fasten off.
3rd rnd: Join D with sl st to any rem loop of 1st rnd. Working in rem loops of 1st rnd, ch 1. *1 sc in next sc. (1 sc. Ch 15. 1 sc) in next sc. Rep from * around. Join with sl st to first sc. (5 ch-15 loops).
4th rnd: *(10 dc. Picot. 10 dc) in next ch-15 sp. Skip next sc. Sl st in next sc. Rep from * around. Fasten off.

FINISHING
Sew Flower to top of Tea Cozy.•

Chart 1
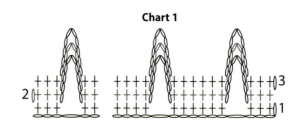

Chart 2
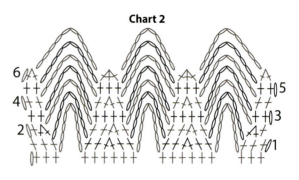

Chart 3
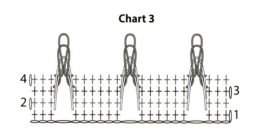

STITCH KEY
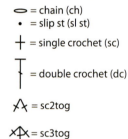
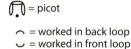

⌒ = worked in back loop
⌣ = worked in front loop

Chart 4
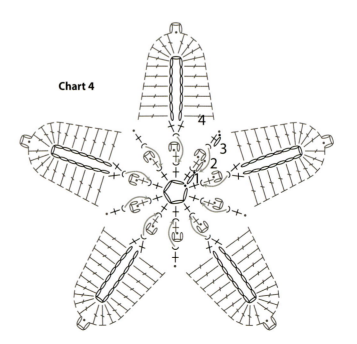

ZIGZAG BLANKET

Easy

MEASUREMENTS
Approx 46"/117cm x 57"/144.5cm

MATERIALS
Yarn (4)
Caron® Simply Soft®, 6oz/170g balls, each approx 315yd/288m (acrylic)
- 6 balls in #9701 White (A)
- 2 balls in #9767 Royal Blue (B)

Yarn (4)
Caron® Simply Soft® Brites™, 6oz/170g balls, each approx 315yd/288m (acrylic)
- 2 balls in #9608 Blue Mint (C)
- 2 balls in #9607 Limelight (D)

Hook
- Size I/9 (5.5mm) crochet hook, *or size needed to obtain gauge*

GAUGE
12 sc and 13 rows = 4"/10cm using size I/9 (5.5mm) hook.
TAKE TIME TO CHECK GAUGE.

NOTES
- First and last sc of each row is left unworked.
- When joining new color, work to last 2 loops on hook of last st. Draw new color through 2 loops, then proceed in a new color.

BLANKET
With A, ch 287. Mark every 50th ch for easier counting.

1st row: (RS) 1 sc in 2nd ch from hook. *(Ch 1. Skip next ch. 1 sc in next ch) 11 times. Ch 2. (1 sc in next ch. Ch 1. Skip next ch) 11 times. 1 sc in next ch.** Skip next 2 ch. 1 sc in next ch. Rep from * 4 times more, then from * to ** once more. Turn. 286 sts.

2nd row: Sl st to first ch-1 sp. Ch 1. 1 sc in same sp as sl st. (Ch 1. Skip next sc. 1 sc in next ch-1 sp) 10 times. Ch 1. *(1 sc. Ch 2. 1 sc) in next ch-2 sp. (Ch 1. Skip next sc. 1 sc in next ch-1 sp) 11 times.** Skip next 2 sc. (1 sc in next ch-1 sp. Ch 1. Skip next sc) 11 times. Rep from * 4 times more, then from * to ** once more. Turn.

Rep last row until work from beg measures 3"/9cm, ending on a WS row.

With B, rep last row for 4"/10cm, ending on a WS row.
With A, rep last row for 3"/9cm, ending on a WS row.
With C, rep last row for 4"/10cm, ending on a WS row.
With A, rep last row for 3"/9cm, ending on a WS row.
With D, rep last row for 4"/10cm, ending on a WS row.
With A, rep last row for 15"/40.5cm, ending on a WS row.
With D, rep last row for 4"/10cm, ending on a WS row.
With A, rep last row for 3"/9cm, ending on a WS row.
With C, rep last row for 4"/10cm, ending on a WS row.
With A, rep last row for 3"/9cm, ending on a WS row.
With B, rep last row for 4"/10cm, ending on a WS row.
With A, rep last row for 3"/9cm, ending on a WS row.
Fasten off.•

RAINBOW STRIPES TABLET & PHONE CASES

Easy

SIZES
Phone Case
To fit device approx 2½"/6cm x 4½"/11.5cm
Tablet Case
To fit device approx 7½"/19cm x 9½"/24cm

MATERIALS
Yarn
Lily® Sugar'n Cream®, 2½oz/71g balls, each approx 120yd/109m (cotton)
Phone Case
- 1 ball in #01740 Hot Pink (A)
- 1 ball in #00095 Red (B)
- 1 ball in #01699 Tangerine (C)
- 1 ball in #01712 Hot Green (D)
- 1 ball in #01742 Hot Blue (E)

Note: 1 ball each of A, B, C, D, and E will make 11 covers.

Tablet Case
- 1 ball in #01740 Hot Pink (A)
- 1 ball in #00095 Red (B)
- 1 ball in #01699 Tangerine (C)
- 1 ball in #01712 Hot Green (D)
- 1 ball in #01742 Hot Blue (E)

Note: 1 ball each of A, B, C, D, and E will make 3 covers.

Hook
- Size E/4 (3.5mm) crochet hook, *or size needed to obtain gauge.*

Notion
- 1 button

GAUGE
16 sc and 17 rows = 4"/10cm using size E/4 (3.5mm) hook.
TAKE TIME TO CHECK GAUGE.

PHONE CASE
Note: Ch 2 at beg of rnds does not count as st.
With A, ch 15.
1st rnd: 1 hdc in 3rd ch from hook. 1 hdc in each of next 11 ch. 3 hdc in last ch. Working across opposite side of foundation ch, 1 hdc in each of next 11 ch. 1 hdc in last ch. Join with sl st to first hdc. 27 sts. Fasten off.
Proceed as follows for rem rnds:
Work hdc in horizontal bar created at back of work between stitches of previous rnd (bar is below loops normally worked—see diagram on page 44). This leaves a "ridge" of top chain across each rnd.
2nd rnd: Join B with sl st in horizontal bar at back of last hdc of previous rnd. Ch 2. 1 hdc in same sp. *1 hdc in horizontal bar at back of next hdc. Rep from * around. Join with sl st to first hdc. Fasten off.
3rd rnd: With C, as 2nd rnd.
4th rnd: With D, as 2nd rnd.
5th rnd: With E, as 2nd rnd.
6th rnd: With A, as 2nd rnd.
Rep 2nd to 6th rnds twice more. Do not fasten off.
Cont as follows for button loop: With A, sl st across each st to center back of last rnd. Ch 24 (button loop). Join with sl st in center back. Fasten off. Sew button to front to correspond to button loop.

TABLET CASE
Notes: This pattern will naturally slant to the bias as you work. It will not affect finished item. Ch 2 at beg of rnds does not count as st.
With A, ch 84. Join in ring with sl st to first ch, taking care not to twist ch.
1st rnd: Ch 2. 1 hdc in first ch. 1 hdc in each of next 2 ch. *Yoh and draw up a loop in next ch. Draw up a loop in each of next 2 ch. Yoh and draw through all 5 loops on hook—hdc3tog made. 1 hdc in each of next 5 ch. 3 hdc in next ch. 1 hdc in each of next 5 ch. Rep

RAINBOW STRIPES TABLET & PHONE CASES

from * to last 11 ch. Hdc3tog. 1 hdc in each of next 5 ch. 3 hdc in next ch. 1 hdc in each of last 2 ch. Join with sl st to first hdc. Fasten off.

Proceed as follows for rem rnds: Work hdc in horizontal bar created at back of work between stitches of previous rnd (bar is below loops normally worked—see diagram below). This leaves a "ridge" of top chains across each rnd.

2nd rnd: Join B with sl st in horizontal bar at back of last hdc of previous rnd. Ch 2. 1 hdc in same sp. Working in horizontal bars created at back of work between stitches of previous rnd, 1 hdc in each of next 2 bars. *Hdc3tog. 1 hdc in each of next 5 bars. 3 hdc in next bar. 1 hdc in each of next 5 bars. Rep from * to last 10 sts. Hdc3tog. 1 hdc in each of next 5 bars. 3 hdc in next bar. 1 hdc in each of last 2 hdc. Join with sl st to first hdc. Fasten off.

3rd rnd: With C, as 2nd rnd.
4th rnd: With D, as 2nd rnd.
5th rnd: With E, as 2nd rnd.
6th rnd: With A, as 2nd rnd.

Rep 2nd to 6th rnds for Stripe Pat until work from beg (measured point to point) measures approx 9"/23cm ending on a 3rd rnd of Stripe Pat.

Next rnd: Join D with sl st in horizontal bar at back of center hdc of last 3 hdc group of previous rnd.

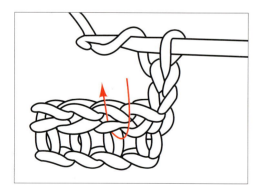

This diagram shows where the horizontal bar is located (on WS of rnd).

Ch 1. 1 sc in same sp. Working in horizontal bars created at back of work between sts of previous rnd, 1 sc in next bar. 1 dc in each of next 3 bars. *[(Yoh) twice and draw up a loop in next bar. (Yoh and draw through 2 loops on hook) twice] 3 times. Yoh and draw through all loops on hook—tr3tog made. 1 dc in each of next 3 bars. 1 hdc in next bar. 1 sc in each of next 3 bars. 1 hdc in next bar. 1 dc in each of next 3 bars. Rep from * to last 8 sts. Tr3tog. 1 dc in each of next 3 bars. 1 hdc in next bar. 1 sc in last bar. Join with sl st to first sc. Do not fasten off.

Button Loop

With C, sl st across to center back of last rnd. Ch 36 (button loop). Join with sl st in center back. Fasten off. Sew button to front to correspond to button loop.

Bottom Edging

Working into rem loops of foundation ch, join E with sl st in any rem loop of center ch of hdc3tog from 1st rnd. Ch 1. 1 sc in same sp. 1 sc in next ch. 1 hdc in next ch. 1 dc in each of next 3 ch. *Tr3tog over next 3 ch. 1 dc in each of next 3 ch. 1 hdc in next ch. 1 sc in each of next 3 ch. 1 hdc in next ch. 1 dc in each of next 3 ch. Rep from * to last 8 ch. Tr3tog over next 3 ch. 1 dc in each of next 3 ch. 1 hdc in next ch. 1 sc in last ch. Join with sl st to first sc. Fasten off.

Join Bottom Edging

Turn work inside out and line up bottom edging. Working through both thicknesses, join E with sl st in corner. Ch 1. 1 sc in same sp. 1 sc in each st across to opposite corner. Fasten off.•

SPECTRUM AFGHAN

Easy

MEASUREMENTS
Approx 54"/137cm wide x 60"/152.5cm long

MATERIALS
Yarn (4)
Caron® Simply Soft®, 6oz/170g balls, each approx 315yd/288m (acrylic)
- 2 balls in #9767 Royal Blue (A)
- 2 balls in #9776 Lemonade (D)
- 2 balls in #9729 Red (F)

Yarn (4)
Caron® Simply Soft® Brites™, 6oz/170g balls, each approx 315yd/288m (acrylic)
- 2 balls in #9608 as Blue Mint (B)
- 2 balls in #9607 as Limelight (C)
- 2 balls in #9605 as Mango (E)

Hook
- Size H/8 (5mm) crochet hook, *or size needed to obtain gauge*

GAUGE
13 hdc and 10 rows = 4"/10cm using size H/8 (5mm) hook.
TAKE TIME TO CHECK GAUGE.

NOTE
- Ch 2 at beg of row counts as hdc throughout.

AFGHAN
With A, ch 196.

1st row: 1 hdc in 3rd ch from hook (counts as 2 hdc). 1 hdc in each ch to end of chain. Turn. 195 hdc.

2nd row: Ch 2. 1 hdc in each st to end of row. Turn. Rep 2nd row, in the following color sequence: *With A, 12 rows. With B, 1 row. With A, 3 rows. With B, 2 rows. With A, 2 rows. With B, 5 rows. With A, 1 row.* Rep from * to * once more, substituting B for A and C for B. Rep from * to * once more, substituting C for A and D for B. Rep from * to * once more, substituting D for A and E for B. Rep from * to * once more, substituting E for A and F for B. With F, work 2 more rows. Fasten off.•

SPIKE-STITCH PILLOW

Easy

MEASUREMENTS
Approx 16"/40.5cm square

MATERIALS
Yarn
Bernat® *Maker Home Dec*™, 8.8oz/250g balls, each approx 317yd/290m (cotton/nylon)
- 1 ball in #11004 Green Pea (A)
- 1 ball in #11006 Steel Blue (B)
- 1 ball in #11001 Woodberry (C)
- 1 ball in #11008 Clay (D)

Hook
- Size K/10½ (6.5mm) crochet hook, *or size needed to obtain gauge*

Notions
- 16"/40.5cm square pillow form
- 1½"/4cm button

STITCH GLOSSARY
Spike St *Insert hook in row indicated and draw up a long loop. Yoh and draw through both loops on hook.*

GAUGE
11 sc and 12 rows = 4"/10cm using size K/10½ (6.5mm) hook. *TAKE TIME TO CHECK GAUGE.*

FRONT
With A, ch 46.

1st row: (RS) 1 sc in 2nd ch from hook. 1 sc in each ch to end of ch. Turn. 45 sc.

2nd row: Ch 1. 1 sc in each sc to end of row. Turn.

3rd and 4th rows: As 2nd row. Join B at end of 4th row.

5th row: With B, ch 1. 1 sc in first sc. *Spike st in next sc 3 rows below. Spike st in next sc 2 rows below. Spike st in next sc 1 row below. 1 sc in next sc. Rep from * to end of row. Turn.

6th row: Ch 1. 1 sc in each st to end of row. Turn.

7th to 9th rows: Ch 1. 1 sc in each sc to end of row. Turn. Join C at end of 9th row.

10th row: (WS) With C, ch 1. 1 sc in first sc. *Spike st in next sc 1 row below. Spike st in next sc 2 rows below. Spike st in next sc 3 rows below. 1 sc in next sc. Rep from * to end of row. Turn.

11th row: As 6th row.

12th to 14th rows: Ch 1. 1 sc in each sc to end of row. Turn. Join D at end of 14th row.

15th row: With D, as 5th row.

16th row: As 6th row.

17th to 19th rows: Ch 1. 1 sc in each sc to end of row. Turn. Join A at end of 19th row.

20th row: With A, as 10th row.

21st row: As 6th row.

22nd to 24th rows: Ch 1. 1 sc in each sc to end of row. Turn. Join B at end of 24th row.

Rep 5th to 24th rows until piece measures approx 16"/40.5cm from beg, ending on a 6th or 11th row. Fasten off.

BACK PIECE (Make 2)
With B, ch 46.

1st row: (RS) 1 sc in 2nd ch from hook. 1 sc in each ch to end of ch. Turn. 45 sc.

2nd row: Ch 1. 1 sc in each sc to end of row. Turn. Rep last row until piece measures approx 10"/25.5cm from beg. Fasten off.

FINISHING
With WS of Front facing up, align 2 Back pieces so that they overlap approx 2"/5cm in the middle. Join B with sl st to any corner. Ch 1. Working through all thicknesses (Front and Back pieces), work 1 rnd of sc evenly around all sides of Pillow, working 3 sc in each corner. Join with sl st to first sc. Fasten off.

Button Loop
Join B with sl st to 23rd sc of one Back piece. Ch 10. Sl st in same sp as last sl st. Fasten off. Sew button on other Back piece to correspond with button Loop. Insert pillow form. Close button loop.●

POP ART FLOWERS BLANKET

Intermediate

MEASUREMENTS
Approx 38"/96.5cm x 47"/119.5cm

MATERIALS
Yarn

Bernat® *Super Value*™, 7oz/197g balls, each approx 426yd/389m (acrylic)
- 1 ball in #53202 Bright Teal (A)
- 1 ball in #00616 Peacock (B)
- 1 ball in #00608 Bright Yellow (C)
- 1 ball in #53417 Peony Pink (D)

Yarn

Bernat® *Pop!*™, 5oz/140g balls, each approx 280yd/256m (acrylic)
- 3 balls in #84001 Scarlett Sizzle (E)
- 3 balls in #84014 Pop Art (F)

Hook
- Size I/9 (5.5mm) crochet hook, *or size needed to obtain gauge*

GAUGE
12 sc and 13 rows = 4"/10cm using size I/9 (5.5mm) hook. *TAKE TIME TO CHECK GAUGE.*

NOTES
- When working 10th to 18th rows from chart, wind small balls of Color 1 to be used, one for each separate area of color in the design. Start new colors at appropriate points.
- When working 1st to 9th rows and 19th to 28th rows from chart, carry colors not in use loosely across top of previous row and work color in use over it. Start new colors at appropriate points.
- To change color, work to last 2 loops on hook. Draw loop of next color through 2 loops on hook to complete st and proceed in next color.

MOTIF
With Color 1, ch 28.

1st row: (RS) 1 sc in 2nd ch from hook and each ch to end of chain. Turn. 27 sc.

2nd row: Ch 1. 1 sc in each sc to end of row. Turn. First 2 rows of chart have been completed. Motif Chart is shown on page 50.
Cont in chart, *reading RS rows from right to left and WS rows from left to right* to end of chart. *Do not* fasten off.

Motif Edging
1st rnd: (RS) With Color 1, ch 1. 3 sc in first sc. 1 sc in each sc to last sc. 3 sc in last sc. *Do not* turn. Work 26 sc down left side of Motif. 3 sc in corner. Work 26 sc in rem loops of foundation ch. 3 sc in corner. Work 26 sc up right side of Motif. Join with sl st to first sc. Fasten off.

Make 5 Motifs having A as Color 1 and F as Color 2.
Make 5 Motifs having B as Color 1 and E as Color 2.
Make 5 Motifs having C as Color 1 and E as Color 2.
Make 5 Motifs having D as Color 1 and F as Color 2.

FINISHING
Following Assembly Diagram on page 50, join Motifs into 4 Strips as follows: With WS tog, *working through both*

POP ART FLOWERS BLANKET

thicknesses, join Color 2 with sl st to corner sc. Ch 1. 1 sc in same sp as sl st. *Ch 2. Skip next 2 sc. *Working through both thicknesses,* 1 sc in next sc. Rep from * to end of row. Fasten off.

Join 4 Strips into Blanket as follows: With WS tog, *working through both thicknesses,* join Color 2 with sl st to corner sc. Ch 1. 1 sc in same sp as sl st. *Ch 2. Skip next 2 sc. *Working through both thicknesses,* 1 sc in next sc.* Rep from * to * to end of Motif. 1 sc in first corner sc of next Motif.** Rep from * to ** to end of row, ending at *. Fasten off.

Edging

1st rnd: (RS) Join A with sl st to corner sc. Work sc evenly around Blanket, having 3 sc in corners. Join B with sl st to first sc.

2nd rnd: With B, ch 1. 1 sc in each sc around, working 3 sc in each corner sc. Join C with sl st to first sc.

3rd rnd: With C, as 2nd rnd. Join with sl st to first sc. Fasten off.•

ASSEMBLY DIAGRAM

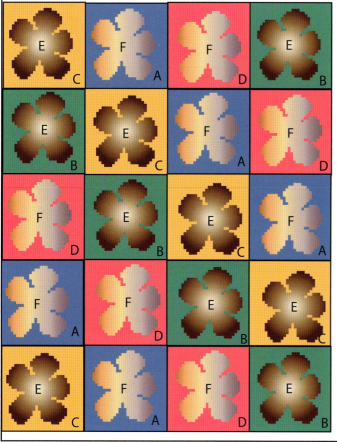

MOTIF CHART

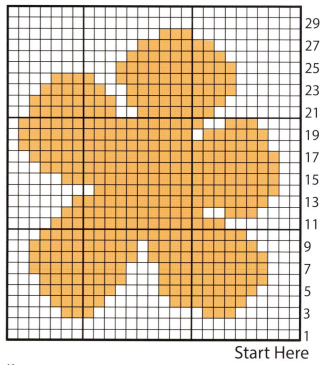

Start Here

Key

☐ = With Color 1, 1 sc

▨ = With Color 2, 1 sc

FLOWER POT COZY

Easy

SIZE
To fit circular plant pot 6¾"/17cm in diameter x 5½"/14cm tall

MATERIALS
Yarn

Phentex® *Slipper and Craft Yarn*, 3oz/85g balls, each approx 164yd/150m (olefin)
- 1 ball in #07712 Hot Lime or #07628 Hot Orange or #00570 Matador or #07332 Grape or #07201 Aqua

Hook
- Size 7 (4.5mm) crochet hook, *or size needed to obtain gauge*

Notion
- 1 stitch marker

GAUGE
15 sc and 16 rows = 4"/10cm using size 7 (4.5mm) hook. *TAKE TIME TO CHECK GAUGE.*

COZY
Ch 4. Join with sl st to first ch to form ring.
1st rnd: Ch 1. 8 sc in ring. Join with sl st to first sc.
2nd rnd: Ch 1. 2 sc in each sc around. Join with sl st to first sc. 16 sc.
3rd rnd: Ch 1. *2 sc in next sc. 1 sc in next sc. Rep from * around. Join with sl st to first sc. 24 sc.
4th rnd: Ch 1. *2 sc in next sc. 1 sc in each of next 2 sc. Rep from * around. Join with sl st to first sc. 32 sc.
5th rnd: Ch 1. *2 sc in next sc. 1 sc in each of next 3 sc. Rep from * around. Join with sl st to first sc. 40 sc.
6th rnd: Ch 1. *2 sc in next sc. 1 sc in each of next 4 sc. Rep from * around. Join with sl st to first sc. 48 sc.
7th rnd: Ch 1. *2 sc in next sc. 1 sc in each of next 5 sc. Rep from * around. Join with sl st to first sc. 56 sc.
8th rnd: Ch 1. *2 sc in next sc. 1 sc in each of next 6 sc. Rep from * around. Join with sl st to first sc. 64 sc.
9th rnd: Ch 1. *2 sc in next sc. 1 sc in each of 7 sc. Rep from * around. Join with sl st to first sc. 72 sc.

Note: To customize size, cont to inc 8 sts each rnd as established until desired diameter for bottom.

Next rnd: Ch 1. *Working in back loops only,* 1 sc in each sc around. Join with sl st to first sc. Place marker at end of rnd.
Next rnd: Ch 1. 1 sc in each sc around. Join with sl st to first sc.
Rep last rnd until work from marked rnd measures 5½"/14cm or desired height. Fasten off.•

STRIPED PLACE SETTING

Easy

MEASUREMENTS
Place Mat
Approx 12"/30.5cm x 18"/45.5cm
Coaster
Approx 5"/12.5cm diameter

MATERIALS
Yarn
Bernat® *Handicrafter*® Cotton, 1¾oz/50g balls, each approx 80yd/73m (cotton)
Place Mats: Set of 2 (Set of 4)
- 2 (4) balls #01742 Hot Blue (A)
- 2 (3) balls #01712 Hot Green (B)
- 2 (3) balls #01628 Hot Orange (C)
- 2 (3) balls #01740 Hot Pink (D)

Napkin Rings and Coasters: Set of 2 (Set of 4)
- 1 (2) ball(s) #01742 Hot Blue (A)
- 1 (1) ball #01712 Hot Green (B)
- 1 (1) ball #01628 Hot Orange (C)
- 1 (1) ball #01740 Hot Pink (D)

Hook
- Size H/8 (5mm) crochet hook, *or size needed to obtain gauge*

GAUGE
14 sc and 16 rows = 4"/10cm using size H/8 (5mm) hook.
TAKE TIME TO CHECK GAUGE.

NOTE
- When changing colors, work to last 2 loops on hook of last st, then draw new color through rem 2 loops and proceed.

PLACE MAT
With A, ch 43.
1st row: (RS) 1 dc in 4th ch from hook (counts as 2 dc). 1 dc in each ch across. 41 sts. Join B. Turn.
2nd row: With B, ch 1. 1 sc in each dc across. Join A. Turn.
3rd row: With A, ch 3 (counts as dc). 1 dc in each sc across. Join B. Turn.
4th row: As 2nd row. Join C. Turn.
5th row: With C, as 3rd row. Join D. Turn.
6th row: With D, as 2nd row. Join C. Turn.
7th row: As 5th row.
8th row: With D, as 2nd row. Join B. Turn.
9th row: With B, as 3rd row. Join A. Turn.
10th row: With A, as 2nd row. Join B. Turn.
11th row: As 9th row.
12th row: With A, as 2nd row. Join D. Turn.
13th row: With D, as 3rd row. Join C. Turn.
14th row: With C, as 2nd row. Join D. Turn.
15th row: As 13th row.
16th row: With C, as 2nd row. Join A. Turn.
17th row: With A, as 3rd row. Join B. Turn.
Rep 2nd to 17th rows for Stripe Pat until work from beg measures approx 18"/45.5cm ending on a 4th or 8th row of pat. Fasten off.

FINISHING
Edging
1st rnd: With RS facing, join A with sl st to any corner of Place Mat and work 1 row of sc evenly around outer edge, working 3 sc in corners. Join with sl st to first sc.
2nd rnd: Ch 1. Working from left to right, instead of from right to left as usual, work 1 reverse sc in each sc around. Join with sl st to first sc. Fasten off.

NAPKIN RING
With B, ch 21.

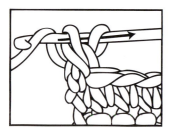 

REVERSE SINGLE CROCHET

1st row: (WS) 1 sc in 2nd ch from hook. 1 sc in each ch across. 20 sts. Join A. Turn.
2nd row: With A, ch 3 (counts as dc). 1 dc in each sc across. Join B. Turn.
3rd row: With B, ch 1. 1 sc in each dc across. Join A. Turn.
4th row: As 2nd row.
5th row: With B, ch 1. 1 sc in each dc across. Fasten off.

FINISHING
Sew sides tog to form ring.

COASTER
With C, ch 2.
1st rnd: 6 sc in 2nd ch from hook. Join with sl st to first sc.
2nd rnd: Ch 1. 2 sc in each sc around. Join with sl st to first sc. 12 sc. Fasten off.

First Petal of Flower
1st row: Join A with sl st to front loop only of any sc. *Ch 1. 2 sc in same sp as sl st. 2 sc in front loop only of next sc. 4 sc for petal. *Turn.*
Next 3 rows: Ch 1. 1 sc in each sc of petal. Turn.
Next row: Ch 1. [*Draw up a loop in each of next 2 sts. Yoh and draw through all 3 loops—sc2tog made*] twice. Fasten off, leaving a long end.*

Second Petal of Flower
Rejoin A with sl st to front loop of next unworked sc of 2nd rnd. Rep from * to * once.

Third to Sixth Petals of Flower
Rep from ** to ** 4 times more. 6 petals.
3rd rnd: Join B with sl st to rem back loop of any sc of 2nd rnd. Ch 3. 1 dc in same sp as sl st. 2 dc in each rem back loop around. Join with sl st to top of ch 3. 24 dc.
4th rnd: Ch 3. 1 dc in same sp as last sl st. *1 dc in next dc. 2 dc in next dc. Rep from * to last dc. 1 dc in last dc. Join with sl st to top of ch 3. 36 dc.
5th rnd: Ch 3. 1 dc in next dc. *2 dc in next dc. 1 dc in each of next 2 dc. 2 dc in next dc. 1 dc in next dc. Rep from * to last 4 dc. 2 dc in next dc. 1 dc in each of next 2 dc. 2 dc in last dc. Join with sl st to top of ch 3. 50 dc.
6th rnd: Ch 1. Working from *left* to right instead of from *right* to left as usual, work 1 reverse sc in each dc around. Join with sl st to first sc. Fasten off.

FINISHING
Using yarn ends from each petal, sew around outer edges of petals.•

LARKSFOOT BLANKET

Easy

MEASUREMENTS
Approx 48"/122cm x 60"/152.5cm

MATERIALS
Yarn (6)

Bernat® *Super Value*™, 7oz/197g balls, each approx 426yd/389m (acrylic)
- 2 balls in #53009 Mushroom (A)
- 1 ball in #53417 Peony Pink (B)
- 1 ball in #00608 Bright Yellow (C)
- 1 ball in #53201 Aqua (D)
- 1 ball in #53725 Hot Blue (E)

Hook
- Size I/9 (5.5mm) crochet hook, *or size needed to obtain gauge*

Notions
Stitch markers

GAUGE
12 dc and 6 rows = 4"/10 cm using size I/9 (5.5mm) hook.
TAKE TIME TO CHECK GAUGE.

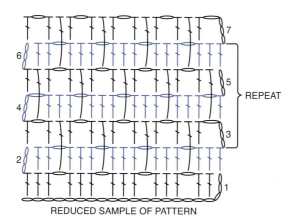

REDUCED SAMPLE OF PATTERN

KEY
- ⌒ = chain (ch)
- ⊤ = double crochet (dc)
- ⊤ = extended double crochet (extended dc)

STITCH GLOSSARY
Stripe Pat
With B, work 2 rows.
With C, work 2 rows.
With A, work 2 rows.
With D, work 2 rows.
With E, work 2 rows.
With A, work 2 rows.
These 12 rows form Stripe Pat.

NOTES
- When joining colors, work to last 2 loops on hook of first color. Draw new color through last 2 loops and proceed.
- Ch 3 at beg of row counts as dc throughout.

BLANKET
With B, ch 145. Mark every 25th ch for easier counting. (See chart.)

1st row: 1 dc in 4th ch from hook (counts as 2 dc). 1 dc in next ch. *Ch 1. Skip next ch. 1 dc in each of next 3 ch. Rep from * to end of chain. Turn.

2nd row: Ch 3. 1 dc in each of next 2 dc. *Ch 1. Skip next ch. 1 dc in each of next 3 dc. Rep from * to end of row. Join C. Turn.

3rd row: With C, ch 4 (counts as dc and ch 1). Skip next dc. 1 dc in next dc. *Yoh and draw up a long loop in ch-1 sp 2 rows below. (Yoh and draw through 2 loops on hook) twice—extended dc made. 1 dc in next dc. Ch 1. Skip next dc. 1 dc in next dc. Rep from * to end of row. Turn.

4th row: Ch 4 (counts as dc and ch 1). Skip next ch. *1 dc in each of next 3 sts. Ch 1. Skip next ch. Rep from * ending with 1 dc in 3rd ch of turning ch. Join A. Turn.

5th row: With A, ch 3. 1 extended dc. 1 dc in next dc. *Ch 1. Skip next dc. 1 dc in next dc. 1 extended dc. 1 dc in next dc. Rep from * to end of row. Turn.

6th row: Ch 3. 1 dc in each of next 2 sts. *Ch 1. Skip next ch. 1 dc in each of next 3 sts. Rep from * to end of row. Join D. Turn.

First 6 rows of Stripe Pat are complete. Rep 3rd to 6th rows until work from beg measures approx 60"/152.5cm, ending with 2 rows of A. Fasten off.•

CHARTS & DIAGRAMS

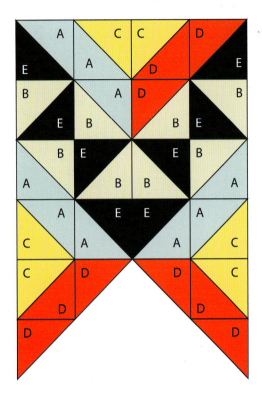

ASSEMBLY DIAGRAM
Geometric Wall Hanging, page 12

SLIP-STITCH DIAGRAM
Citrus Slice Rug, page 24

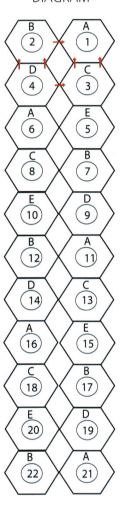

ASSEMBLY DIAGRAM

Flower Power
Table Runner,
page 32

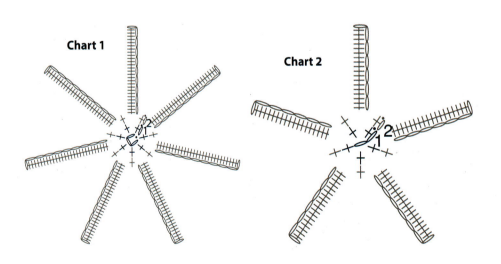

Bouquet Baskets,
page 18